Corporate Planning
and Control Model Systems

Corporate Planning and Control Model Systems

Akira Ishikawa

Graduate School of Business Administration
New York University

New York: NEW YORK UNIVERSITY PRESS ● 1975

59805

Copyright © 1975 by New York University

Library of Congress Catalog Card Number: 75-13745
ISBN: 0-8147-3751-X

Library of Congress Cataloging in Publication Data

Ishikawa, Akira, 1934-
  Corporate Planning and Control Model Systems

  Bibliography: p.
  1. Industrial management—Mathematical Models.
2. Corporations—Mathematical models. I. Title.
HD20.4.I83   658.4   75-13745
ISBN 0-8147-3751-X

To my parents

CONTENTS

PREFACE

A number of major corporations (organizations) in the United States, Canada, Europe, Latin America, and Japan are using or developing corporate (organizational) planning and control models, with an increasing awareness and conviction among corporate (organizational) executives and planners that such vital issues as the energy crisis, raw material shortages, unemployment, pollution, declining productivity, and interdependence require a more systematic and overall approach to corporate (organizational) planning and control that should differ substantially from traditional seat-of-the-pants techniques. In other words, computerized and noncomputerized corporate models are required to provide the tools to understand our environment and forecast ways to control that environment, in addition to solving the problems internal to the corporation.

The theme of this book is to meet these important and imminent requirements by overviewing the present state of corporate planning and corporate models (chapters 1 and 2), suggesting the steps to be taken to develop the models (chapter 3), identifying the main problems involved in the development of corporate models and suggesting solutions to these problems (chapter 4), providing with the potential and available techniques in improving and expanding the models (chapter 5), and reviewing the future potential of corporate (organizational) planning and control models (chapter 6) mainly from the standpoints of *model users*.

This book is designed therefore, for those who run a gamut from laymen . . . , including business and public administration and computer sciences students who will be and are interested in modeling and simulation, to computer and information planners and specialists; they include administrators, corporate planners, financial analysts, accountants, controllers, system analysts, information system specialists, and operations research specialists, etc.

Note, however, that the author has purposely excluded the basic technical backgrounds, such as the details of program languages, operating systems, computer files, and hardware components that readers can easily gain access to through standard texts in the field of information systems and/or computer systems.

This text has been utilized as one of the primary texts for a one-semester course at the Graduate School of Business Administration, New York University. The only prerequisite was a one-semester course entitled Computer-Based Information Systems, in which an introduction to computers and applications is covered, including the topics mentioned above. At NYU, however, some students have usually taken two or more courses in the field of Computer Applications and Information Systems. Another group of students have already gained enough experience as a system programmers, system analysts, computer specialists, or computer system managers before taking this course. Under such circumstances, this text has also been used as a reference or a guideline in order to develop modeling projects by groups.

Since an intermediate or an advanced course of information and computer systems and modeling is required to be designed as flexibly as possible, with emphasis on either model systems users or builders, or both, additional references are given in the Bibliography and related references, and supplementary readings are provided at the end of each chapter, so that the instructor may place emphasis on certain topics, depending upon his or her value judgment.

The review questions and problems at the end of each chapter are designed to determine the degree of understanding and incite discussion. Although answers to the questions and problems are for the most part provided, the student is urged to consult with the recommended relevant readings to broaden and deepen understanding of the subject matter. Certain questions and problems (marked with an asterisk) indicate their suitability for a term project.

I would like to express my appreciation to numerous people for their assistance and guidance in the many stages of preparation of this book, especially to Dean George Kozmetsky, professors Thomas H. Williams, Abraham Charnes, and Michael Duggan of The University of Texas at Austin, Professor Charles H. Smith of Arizona State University, Professor Richard C. Larson of MIT, Professor Joseph San Miguel of Harvard University, Professor John Buckley of UCLA, Professor Nicholas Dupoch of the University of Chicago, Dr. Thomas Naylor of Social Systems, Inc. and Duke University, Professor Louis Davidson of the University of North Carolina, Professor Martin Starr of Columbia University, the late Mr. John C. Fraser and Mr. Joel C. Magyar of the New York Life Insurance Company, Mr. John Lastavica of the First National Bank of Boston, Mr. J.W. Kroeger of the Lockheed-Georgia Company, Mr. David E. Besenfelder of the Wells Fargo Bank, Mr. J.B. Sloat of the Ford Motor Company, and Dr. Virgil R. Rehg of the Department of the Air Force, Dean William R. Dill, and professors Myron Uretsky, Henry C. Lucas, Jr. Melvin Shakun and Lee J. Seidler of New York University. I would also like to thank the many persons who helped me prepare this text for publication. Geryl Strumpf and Alice Jarvis were responsible for typing and revising the early and successive versions of the manuscript. Mr. Robert Bull and Ms. Despina Papazoglou of NYU Press made many constructive comments and suggestions during the final stage of preparation.

I am also indebted to those of my students and colleagues who read and made critical review on the manuscript. Professors Larry Rosenberg's and Martin Holley's comments were particularly helpful in revision of the manuscript. Finally, I would like to thank my wife, Minako, whose encouragement, enthusiasm, and patience made the book possible.

—Akira Ishikawa

FOREWORD

The nature of my calling demands my constant application to all accessible materials written on the unceasing development in the field of business administration and related disciplines. Among varied and surprisingly diversified maturation, the impact of computers and related science and technology in private and public organizations has been really noteworthy. This became particularly evident in the 1950's and expanded in the 1960's. By the dawn of 1970, we could foresee that one of the most important subjects of this decade would be the intelligent application of computers coping with the kaleidoscopic changes taking place in private and public organizations.

Professor Ishikawa, one of my former students, has dedicated himself wholeheartedly to this vital theme and applied himself vigorously to meet its challenge. To preserve valuable research, his findings were incorporated into a book. This book is a tentative, but well sought outcome derived from his continual endeavors in private, public, and educational institutions.

Because I know Professor Ishikawa to be a dedicated man versed in his subject, I strongly recommend this book. Administrators, executives, specialists, engineers, controllers, accountants, students, and would-be students in the fields of computers, business, and public administration will find in its pages a fund of knowledge, a vital instrument in the advancement of their careers and furthermore of their professions.

Abraham Charnes
Jesse H. Jones Professor
of Biomathematics and Management
Science, Director, Center for
Cybernetic Studies, and The
University of Texas System
Professor

CHAPTER I

Introduction

Business organizations have been involved in countless efforts to improve corporate and budgetary planning, organization, and control, especially in order to cope with and overcome severe declines in economic activity. Generally stated, firms need to anticipate internal and external changes, discover the best alternatives for accomplishing organizational objectives, and initiate actions which would enable them and the economy to attain normal economic growth.

One effective approach to a solution of this problem is the development of organizational (corporate) planning and control models, particularly corporate financial models. In the face of changing internal and external (environmental) factors, such models permit management to:

1. Set new corporate goals.
2. Evaluate alternative courses of action.
3. Analyze the effect of interacting internal and external factors.
4. Validate conventionally prepared forecasts and procedures.
5. Identify quite specifically what planning action (initiative) is required.
6. Develop a management information system or subsystems.[1]
7. Reduce response time against kaleidoscopic changes.

Focus on such models has included the development of appropriate computer-based models for individual departments and/or divisions as well as for the corporation as a whole. The more recent models have tended to be larger in organizational coverage (one is able to observe an evolution from divisional to corporate models[2] and also from corporate to interindustry models[3] and large-scale storage devices,[4] and more responsive[5] in terms of time and number of alternatives considered. They have also included the use of audio or visual devices,[6] that can generate more intelligent outputs with an increasing reduction in input.

Although progress has been made in a number of different directions by individual model builders, there is a lack of comparative analysis of these efforts. It is anticipated that more and more organizations are going to want to develop

1

models of their own, and this comparative analysis could conceivably draw attention to the main problem areas and potential solutions.

Furthermore, despite the progress to date, most models do not lend themselves to the immediate solution of numerous technical problems, such as the identification of user information preferences, use of additional management science techniques, and provision of a basis for validating the model.

SPECIFIC OBJECTIVES OF THIS TEXT

It is the objective of this text to:
1. Provide a background and instructions for the general approach to developing corporate planning and control models.
2. Identify the main problems involved in the development of corporate planning and control models, and to suggest solutions to these problems.
3. Suggest approaches to the solution of a number of specific problems which existing models do not appear to have solved. The problems to be studied are: (a) identification of user information requirements, (b) provision of a basis for validating models, (c) application of management science techniques.

METHODOLOGY AND ORGANIZATION PLAN

The first objective will be accomplished by undertaking a thorough, comparative analysis of modeling and modeling-related research efforts to date. This analysis will include reference to the research efforts of the author which have concerned the development of corporate (financial) planning and control models for several manufacturing and service corporations, and for public agencies.

This comparative analysis enables the reader to:
1. Identify and explain the matters that require attention when studying, evaluating, and developing corporate models (Chapter II).
2. Outline the actual process of constructing a model (Chapter III).
3. Clarify exactly what model users, particularly, corporate executives can expect from corporate models, and to outline specific considerations for ensuring acquisition of such benefits (Chapter IV).

The second objective will be accomplished by describing approaches used by the author and others in practice (a and b of the third objective), and by describing selected techniques which, as a result of work on an actual model and other research, the author believes have significant application potential (c of the third objective).

The user information requirements problem is covered as an integral part of the discussions of chapters II to IV, and in Chapter V it is solved by the priority matrix and interval analysis techniques.

The development of a basis for validating a model is covered as an integral part of Chapter II. Four potential benefits from corporate models are developed and discussed in Chapter IV. These benefits may also be used as a basic set of criteria for validating the model. The interval analysis technique suggested in Chapter V is also discussed as one means of developing such a basis.

Three management science techniques are discussed in Chapter V: the feedforward control, priority matrix, and interval analysis. They are used in the models developed by the author and their application and potential extensions are discussed.

There are a number of problems that do not lend themselves to immediate solution. In Chapter VI there is a summary of the study and conclusions that can be drawn therefrom. A few general suggestions as to approaches for solution of especially complex problems are made. However, these suggestions are not the result of in-depth research, and the approaches will require much further investigation, study, and research. Appendix 4 is an illustration of the questionnaire to study further present state of the arts in corporate models designed by Robert Stein, one of the MBA students at the Graduate School of Business Administration, New York University. This questionnaire has already been sent to about 500 major corporations in the U.S., Europe, and Japan. The report will be published separately.

GLOSSARY

Fundamental and important terms that appear frequently in this text are defined as follows:

Models: A system of postulates, hypotheses, information, data, and inferences delineated as a descriptive, predictive, and/or normative representation of reality or the state of affairs. Models are designed and constructed for purposes of solving both simple and complicated problems of real life, as a system of imitation, simulation, and abstraction of reality. Therefore, models can be classified differently, depending upon different taxonomical schemes. Based upon structures, for example, we have iconic, analog, and symbolic models, whereas on uncertainty references, deterministic, probabilistic, and game theory models. (For more details, see, for example, Murdick and Ross [13], pp. 379-85.) In this text, we are basically concerned with computer or computerized models which are defined as logical or mathematical models expressed specifically by a set of rules in order that they may be processed through a computer. The term "Model System" connotes a system of models, in which model users, hardware, software, and interface components are included, as is shown in Appendix 3.

Corporate Models: Those models which are designed exclusively for accomplishing corporate objectives. They include all the means and vehicles artificially designed through a scientific approach that can be utilized by management or a model user for fulfilling varied business functions and making decisions. Ordinarily, they are logically designed, mathematically formulated, and realistically patterned. They have been increasingly computerized and deal principally with corporate-level planning, organization, and control rather than divisional- or departmental-level functions. When we simply say "corporate models," they are assumed to achieve overall and aggregate corporate functions, not an independent business function, such as production, personnel, accounting, finance, etc. It should, therefore, be noted that corporate models are frequently assumed to be composed of a certain number of submodels, for example, econometric, simulation, optimization, and also information generation and retrieval that should function at times independently or interdependently to achieve aggregate corporate objectives. In appendixes 1, 2, and 3, actual corporate models (systems) are attached.

Corporate (Organizational) Planning and Control Models: A more specific expression on corporate (organizational) models with emphasis on planning and control function of a corporation (organization). In a broader sense, corporate planning and control models is a synonym for corporate models. Strictly stated, however, the former is a submodel of the latter which should encompass other functions, for example, coordinating, organizing, recording, reporting, and evaluating. Since most of the functions aforementioned can be represented by planning and control functions, and since our modeling efforts have frequently been centered around planning (and control), the term "corporate planning models" has been widely utilized rather than "corporate planning and control models".

Financial Planning (and Control) Model (Corporate Financial Model): This is a model designed and constructed specifically for the purpose of aiding in the financial planning of a corporation. Therefore, this model is in essence a submodel of the corporate planning and control model, comparable with production planning, inventory planning, personnel planning, and R & D planning models in terms of the functional level of the firm. Because financial planning is vital for the survival and growth of the corporation, more attention has been given recently to the development of a computerized financial planning (and control) model, as compared with a computerized production planning or inventory planning model that attention was called to in the 1960s.

On-Line Model (Interactive Model): The nature of this model is to provide response to a model user with the minimal time delay or interactively, so that immediate planning decision and control can be made whenever required. This model is viewed as an extended version of an off-line model where a considerable time delay for obtaining a response is inevitable. With reduced costs associated with their use, more models have been designed and constructed as interactive and employed through terminals with and/or without a display device. When a model is used through the terminal with the display device, it is called "interactive graphics model".

The FORPLANCON Model: The author has developed a corporate financial model (FORPLANCON) for a major U.S. insurance company (INCO).[6] FOR-

PLANCON is an aggregative model (with simulation and optimization features) of financial planning, staffing requirements, and control of INCO's divisional operations. Particular attention was given for the model to review appropriately annual budgetary planning to be prepared by each division manager.

The comparative analysis of this study includes frequent reference to FORPLANCON and other models for illustrative purposes.

SUPPLEMENTARY READINGS

1. Churchill, N., Kempster, J., and Uretsky, M. *Computer-Based Information Systems for Management: A Survey*. New York: National Association of Accountants, 1969.
2. Gershefski, George W. "Corporate Models—The State of the Art," in Schrieber, Albert N., ed., *Corporate Simulation Models*. Seattle, Washington: University of Washington, 1970, 26-42.
3. Green, R. Elliot, and Parslow, R.D., eds. *Computer Graphics in Management*. London: Gower Press Limited, 1970.
4. Murray, Gordon L. A 1970-Model Planning, Control, and Information System. New York: Haskins and Sells, 1969.
5. Naylor, Thomas H. *Computer Simulation Experiments with Models of Economic Systems*. New York: John Wiley & Sons, Inc., 1971, chapters 3 and 4.
6. Reitman, Julian. *Computer Simulation Applications*. New York: Wiley-Interscience, 1971.

REVIEW QUESTIONS AND PROBLEMS

1. What would be some effective approaches to the problems of anticipating internal and external changes within a firm, discovering the best alternatives for accomplishing organizational objectives, and initiating actions which would enable the company and the economy to attain normal economic growth?

2. What references do you need to observe the evolution and development of organizational planning and control models?

3. Describe what organizational (corporate) planning and control models permit management to function effectively.

4. Summarize the characteristics of the more recent models in terms of organizational coverage, responsiveness, and the use of audio-visual devices.

5. Despite the fact that progress has been made in a number of different directions by individual model builders, what problems remain to be solved?

6. Elucidate some of the essential problems which exist, but are unsolvable soon in most models.

7. How do you evaluate the present utilization of computers in meeting management's information needs?

*8. What kind of study plan would you design if you were asked to evaluate varied corporate planning and control models?

*9. What are your principal aims in the above study? Discuss your priorities in relation to your expected findings.

*10. Give a detailed outline of the procedures you will employ in your study.

NOTES

1. This is more likely to be the case in an organization that has computer facilities. In a recent survey, the users of management information systems representing 655 firms (73 percent of those responding) indicated that their companies had not utilized computers to maximum advantage in meeting management's information needs. See Barnett [1] * for details.

2. For instance, see Gershefski [2] and [3], as well as the proceedings of conferences at Duke University [4], the University of Texas at Austin [5], and the University of Washington [6]. See also the proceedings of conferences on simulation or computer sciences sponsored by the Association for Computing Machinery, American Institute of Industrial Engineers, Society to Help Avoid Redundant Effort, The Institute of Management Sciences, Society for computer Simulation, and American Federation of Information Processing Societies as well as relevant publications by computer and modeling services organizations, such as the Service Bureau Corporation, Social Systems, Inc., and Management Science of America, Inc., to name a few.

3. For instance, see Seitz [7].

4. This necessitates intelligent management of very large data bases.

5. For example, such models as FAPS (Financial Analysis and Planning System) by On-Line Decisions, Inc. Some of the corporate models developed by On-Line Decisions, Inc., are linked through a computer to the econometric model from which they take their inputs. See Boulden [8] and Wagle [9].

6. See Miller [10] and Shostack and Eddy [11].

*Each number in brackets corresponds with the number of the bibliography by chapters. (See Page 139. It is suggested for the reader to refer to these references before looking at supplementary readings attached to each chapter.)

Appendix

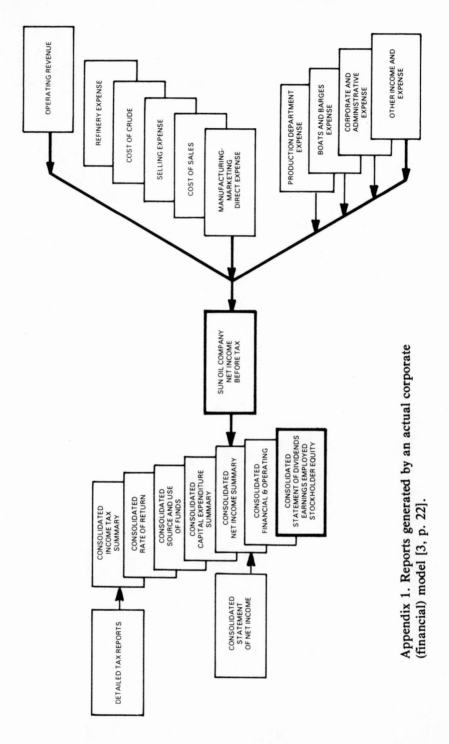

Appendix 1. Reports generated by an actual corporate (financial) model [3, p. 22].

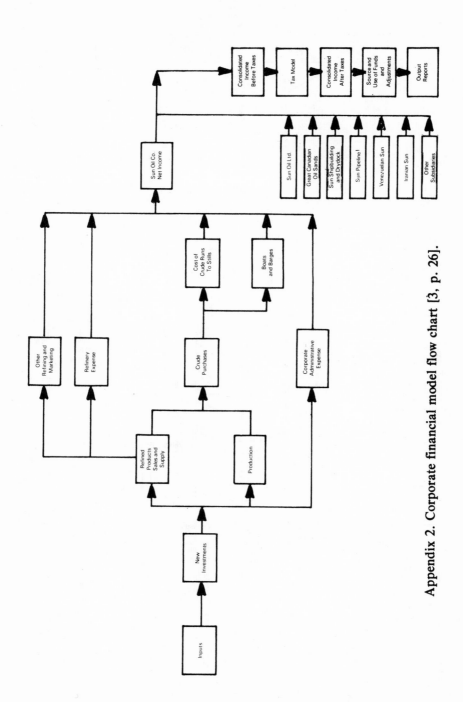

Appendix 2. Corporate financial model flow chart [3, p. 26].

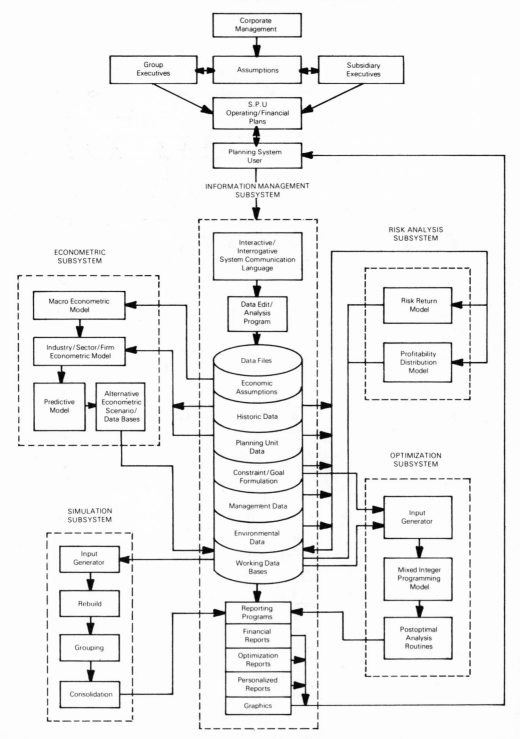

Appendix 3. IV International corporate planning (model) system [12, p. 152].

APPENDIX 4. COMPUTERIZED CORPORATE PLANNING MODELS

Introduction

1-1   What kind of model is being used? Check one.
      (a)   1. Computer
           2. Manual
           3. Both

      (b)   1. Probabilistic
           2. Deterministic
           3. Both

      (c)   1. On-line
           2. Off-line
           3. Both

      (d)   1. Interactive
           2. Noninteractive
           3. Both

1-2   How many computerized models do you have? Check one.
      (a)   One

      (b)   More than one

      (c)   Zero

1-3   What are the types of the model (or models if more than one model)?
      Check as many as are applicable.
      (a)   Functional
           1. Marketing
           2. Production
           3. Accounting
           4. Personnel
           5. Other–explain ⎯⎯⎯⎯⎯⎯⎯⎯⎯⎯⎯⎯

      (b)   Divisional–explain ⎯⎯⎯⎯⎯⎯⎯⎯⎯⎯⎯⎯

      (c)   Geographic
           1. International
           2. National
              (1) Regional (2) State (3) Country (4) City
           3. Other–explain ⎯⎯⎯⎯⎯⎯⎯⎯⎯⎯⎯⎯

Development of Model

1-4   Have the information requirements been given by
      (a)   The model users?
      (b)   The model builders?
      (c)   Interaction between model users and builders?

(d)   Interaction between model users, builders, and agent? Check a, b, c, or d. (Internal or External Coordinators)

1-5   Who is the ultimate model user? Check a, b, c, or d.
   (a)   Top management
   (b)   Middle management
   (c)   Lower management
   (d)   Combination of a, b, & c. Explain _____

1-6   What was the first developed approach in using the model? Check a, b, or c.
   (a)   Top-down approach
   (b)   Bottom-up approach
   (c)   Eclectic approach

1-7   As a corollary to (6), did the corporation change the approach after it was first developed? Check yes or no.

   Yes ___   No ___

1-8   If yes, how? Explain _____

1-9   How often do you use the corporate model for its intended purpose?
   (a)   Every week
   (b)   Every month
   (c)   Every three months
   (d)   Every six months
   (e)   other–explain _____

1-10 Has it functioned well? Answer yes or no.

   Yes ___   No ___

1-11 Is top management the sole user. Answer yes or no.

   Yes ___   No ___

1-12 If the answer to question (10) is no, does the model's use include middle and lower management? Answer yes or no.

   Yes ___   No ___

Internal Factors Affecting Model's Use
2-1   Is the model used for simulation or optimization? Answer one.
   (a)   Simulation ___

   (b)   Optimization ___

   (c)   Other. Explain _____

2-2   To what extent has the model contributed to corporate planning?
Check one.
  (a)   Very much _____
  (b)   Somewhat _____
  (c)   Little _____
  (d)   None _____

2-3   What is the model's (or models') goal? Check those that apply.
  (a)   New Products _____
  (b)   New Processes _____
  (c)   Improved Products _____
  (d)   Improved Processes _____
  (e)   Other. Explain _____

2-4   If either b or d was checked, what is the model's (or models') specific
goal? Check those that apply.
  (a)   Evaluate alternative strategies (Investment, managerial and
        operational).
  (b)   Provide financial projections more frequently.
  (c)   Aid in determining feasible corporate goals.
  (d)   Analyze the effect of interacting factors.
  (e)   Assess sensitivity of earnings to the change of external factors.
  (f)   Other. Explain _____

2-5   As you developed the model did you find new management science
techniques or extend old management techniques? Explain.

        Yes _____   No _____

2-6   If in questions 2-5 you developed new techniques, what are they? Explain.

2-7   Have you changed the corporate model's (or models') objectives? Check
yes or no.

        Yes _____   No _____

If yes, identify the costs that have increased.

2-9   How has the corporate model benefited you? Check all applicable answers.
  (a)   Increase sales
  (b)   Decrease costs
  (c)   Increase return on investment
  (d)   Other, specify _____

2-10 What, if any, percentage increase in return on investment occurred from model's (models') use? Explain _____

External Factors Affecting Model

3-1 How have all the recent problems such as the energy crisis, population explosion, environmental pollution, and unemployment been internalized and considered by the corporation in its planning policy? Explain for each.
    (a) Energy Crisis
    (b) Environmental Pollution
    (c) Population Explosion
    (d) Economic Indices (i.e., unemployment rate)

3-2 To what extent has the corporation used its planning model in weighting these recent problems?
    (a) All the time
    (b) Most of the time
    (c) Some of the time
    (d) Rarely
    (e) Never

3-3 If you do not weight these factors now, do you plan to internalize the functions in the future? Answer yes or no.

        Yes ____   No ____

3-4 Have you internationalized the corporate planning model (models) to feed into international systems such as consolidation, tax problems, investment, or other? Explain for each,
    (a) Consolidation
    (b) Tax Problems
    (c) Investment
    (d) Other

3-5 Do you have sufficient capacity for maintenance and retrieval? Explain.

Other Comments

4-1 You may use this space for further comments on you corporate planning model. Your comments will be greatly appreciated.

CHAPTER II

Fundamental Characteristics
of Corporate Models—An Overview

The salient attempt of this chapter is to elucidate the main elements of corporate models in general through a comparative analysis of various corporate models. The taxonomical scheme employed identifies the main elements of corporate models; they are objectives, scope, design methods, users and uses, information requirements, data management, and management science techniques employed.

The elements are fundamental for the following reasons: (1) In designing, constructing, and evaluating corporate models, most builders or users identify and contend with these topics.[1] (2) The user's or builder's understanding of these topics determines the success or failure of their corporate models.[2]

OBJECTIVES

Each corporate model has particular objectives, according to the peculiar needs of the business it is designed to serve.[3]

From the corporate point of view, the corporate model should be designed and constructed to support the ultimate objective of a corporation. It is not so facile as may appear to state the ultimate objective pragmatically. Profit-making, while a common objective of nearly all corporations, is naturally too broad and abstract for use in setting objectives of corporate models.

It is necessary for model builders and users, and mediating agents between them, therefore, to analyze this general objective into more specific objectives, so that corporate models contribute through these objectives to profit-making. In other words, objectives should be stated operationally, verifiably realistic and attainable, and must take into account the future so as to remain valid in the continuous process of organizational activities. If a hierarchy of objectives must be determined it should be well ordered and relationships clearly identified. Objectives of corporate models are found in the answers to this question: "*Why* and *to what extent* should corporate models be constructed?"

15

A *partial* answer to this query is given by Gershefski's survey of corporate models.[4] According to its results, "To evaluate *alternative* operating or investment strategies" was mentioned thirty times, the highest frequency, equivalent to 17.6 percent, in replies from a wide variety of 323 industries. However, this objective is not overwhelming in comparison to others mentioned, such as "To provide revised financial projections rapidly" (12.9 percent), "To assist in determining feasible corporate goals" (11.8 percent), "To analyze the effect of interacting items" (11.8 percent), "To determine sensitivity of earnings to external factors" (10.0 percent), "To develop a documented projection of financial position" (9.4 percent), and "To allow management to consider more variables when planning" (9.4 percent), in terms of the frequency. The other objectives mentioned in the survey, "To determine manually prepared projections and existing procedures" (8 percent), and "To assist in the evaluation of capital investment proposals" (5 percent), are also worth noting, since they reveal management attitudes toward applying corporate models to financial planning, validation, and information systems.

In addition to the results of the above survey, a corporate model can also be used to determine feasible corporate goals. Since a firm has varied goals, that is, strategic, tactical, managerial, operational, and technical, corporate models must be made sufficiently flexible to examine diverse corporate activities. Therefore the following conclusions are drawn:

1. In the present framework of corporate models, the meaning and place of model objectives are identified more concretely and operationally than in traditional statements of corporate objectives such as maximizing profit,[5] satisficing goals[6] or organizational survival.[7]
2. Corporate models are largely "Corporate Financial Planning Models."[8]
3. Corporate models are sought as a means of rapidly generating alternatives for planning decisions.
4. Corporate models are also constructed as a means of analyzing, evaluating, and determining planning alternatives.
5. Ninety-four percent of corporate models are computerized, according to Gershefski's survey.[9]

Another interpretation of why corporate models are constructed is provided by the approach of Glans, Grad, Holstein, Meyers, and Schmidt.[10] They define goals (objectives) as "the contributions a business wishes to make to its environment." Accordingly, "goals are precisely spelled out, concrete objectives of the business, based on *definite* statements of what the business system must accomplish." They emphasize that "goal definition, good or bad, may predetermine the final system design since activities are keyed to it."[11]

A definitive statement of the objectives of a corporation is inevitably required for the design, construction, and evaluation of corporate models. And a specific statement of model objectives, in turn, helps the model user evaluate the feasibility of corporate objectives. Therefore, even if the initial motive of a firm is not to examine but to execute objectives through corporate models, the necessity of reexamining corporate goals is frequently revealed through the exchange of information between model builders and users. Some clear examples of this benefit are shown by Glans, Grad, Holstein, Meyers, and Schmidt,[12] and Ishikawa.[13]

In one example, the primary objective of a model, "To help an executive simulate financial planning, staffing requirements, and control of each division through printed outputs or display screens," was transformed into more technical, secondary objectives, such as the following:

1. Predicting production, expenses, and staffing for the near future.
2. Maximizing production with variable expenses and staffing constraints.
3. Minimizing expenses and staffing with variable production constraints.[14]
4. Answering "what if" type questions on an on-line basis, through a terminal or display equipment.

Thus, corporate goals can be examined in terms of objective-setting (establishment of objectives), objectives execution, and objectives improvement or refinement.[15]

SCOPE

The functional scope of a corporate model must be defined if the objectives it establishes for the business are to be feasible. Also, a definite scope limits the range of derivable objectives. On the other hand, corporate obectives and the scope of the corporate model have a mutually delimiting relationship.

The establishment of the scope of operation of a corporate model, therefore, determines the limits within which the model must be designed and constructed to achieve the objectives of the corporation.

System researchers may regard this as part of the broader problem of system task requirements or activity structure.[16]

In order to define the scope of the model (and corporate objectives), certain information must be obtained, including the present and future nature of the environment in which the model functions; the organizational characteristics of the company, including its decision-making processes, and general and specific information flows; and revealed and potential management problems. Specific decision-making processes, and corresponding information flows in the area in which the model is to be applied, should be especially reviewed. Since the model is primarily utilized for the purpose of forecasting, planning, budgeting, and controlling, the mechanism of financial or budgetary planning and control should be fully understood.

In addition to the considerations aforementioned, additional informal and intangible factors, that is corporate traditions, informal power structures, and so forth, must be considered to establish a workable and feasible scope within which the model can function to achieve its objectives.

Approaches to scope setting, evaluation, and revision have been made from the perspective of operations, timing, and users. These three approaches are examined in some detail below.

Operations

The corporate model can be applied to a certain corporate operation or operations. Operations can be broadly interpreted as such functions as accounting, finance, marketing, personnel, etc. The operations of a geographically dispersed organization must be considered on a geographical basis. For example, Abe organizes operations according to business lines, such as service stations, consumer products, fuel oil, and others. These business lines are then incorporated in his cascading system which is subordinate to geographical considerations.[17] The Xerox planning model, on the other hand, remains a planning tool within the Business Products Group of the Xerox Corporation.[18] Also, in the early stage of its development, FORPANCON was applied to continuous policy operations.[19]

Note, however, that a corporate model largely consists of several submodels, and therefore several functions could define its total scope. The following statement by Chambers et al. describes a typical example.

Accordingly, an initial set of assumptions and estimates is made to generate inputs for one or more of the models, e.g., the marketing and short-term planning models, and the outputs for these models then generate inputs for the plant location model, which provides inputs for the risk-analysis model which generates new inputs for the short-term planning model, and so forth.[20]

In this instance, the scope covers the functions of marketing, plant locating, and finance.

More extensive coverage of functions can be observed in the corporate model of the New York Life Insurance Company, with its complicated linkage of submodels. Fraser says that "as time goes by and our corporate model [consisting of thirty-seven submodels] evolves, we will make more and more linkages between input data by constructing additional submodels. Sensitivity testing of the entire corporate model will tell us the most important linkages that still need to be made and we will try to deal with these first."[21] However, he doubts the value of the unending increase of submodels:

I suspect that 25 years from now our company model may consist of over 1,000 submodels and that it will still not be satisfactory in the eyes of those using it.[22]

Model builders seek to increase the number of operations and to explore and identify key relationships among various operations or functions,[23] in order to increase its possible productive applications, as well as to acquire personal competence in using the model.

Timing

Any model development plan includes consideration of timing requirements.

The scope of the model is established and revised to meet the needs of management decision making when those needs arise, instead of accomodating operational requirements. For example, even if the establishment of a long-term financial planning model is of greater ultimate value, a short-term financial planning model would be established first, because it would be used to make necessary decisions before the former would be useful. In the initial stage of model development this "Let's-begin-with-the-thing-which-is-in-time" approach has been frequently adopted. Further consideration is given to this approach in the next chapter.

User

Approaches to scope setting, evaluation, and revision of corporate models must directly or indirectly take into account the particular information requirements of the user. The characteristics and coverages of specific models are necessarily different because of the different users they serve, for example, a president vs. a financial analyst. Generally, as users' needs become more specific or fewer in number, the function of the model becomes more specific, and therefore its scope reflects users' special interests, as pointed out by Gaylord A. Freeman, Jr.[24] Further discussion of the influence of users also appears in the next chapter.

DESIGN METHODS

After the objectives and scope of a model have been clarified, methods of establishing (basic design approach) and improving it must be determined. The methods most commonly used by model builders are top-down, bottom-up, and eclectic.

Top-down Approach

The top-down approach places a higher priority on the information requirements of top management than on those of middle or low management in designing, constructing, and refining the corporate model. The model is used by top management people and information flows from top to bottom. Its focus is the corporation as a whole.

For instance, the company model of the Lockheed-Georgia Company assists top executives in evaluating each planning problem and selecting the best solution. Furthermore, this model "assists top management in evaluating the effects of events and changes on company financial and manpower requirements."[25] Since company summary reports are more important than detailed reports to support the summary, the detailed reports are optional output and the user of the model may suppress them by specifying the appropriate options.

It is therefore characteristic of the top-down approach to determine the *sum* before identifying each independent segment, that is, to determine corporate requirements before identifying each divisional requirementt.

Another example of the top-down approach, showing the influence of top management on use of the model, is the "Banker" model of the First National Bank of Boston. Lastavica says:

> ... doing it via the model route gave us the assurance that we were much more thorough in evaluating various interactions than we would have been otherwise. Significantly, it was the *Chairman* who requested that we evaluate the proposition via the model, which indicates that we have gained his confidence.[26]

Although observation of at least two hundred different corporate models has shown that the top-down approach tends to generate specific outputs which are not necessarily related to formal financial statements[27] (for example, balance sheet, income statement, statement of retained earnings, and of cash flows), this "Banker" model puts out a pro forma balance sheet, ratio balance sheet, and income statement, and similar financial statements. While this approach has the strength of showing the influence of top management, some weaknesses are summarized below:

1. Information requirements cannot be transformed into technical and internal requirements easily. (If accomplished, it takes more time.)

2. Organization of an appropriate task force is more difficult, once the need arises. (If organized, it would take time and the less initiative.)

3. A logical process, in a narrow sense, cannot be followed. (Information requirements are likely to be changed more frequently.)

Bottom-up Approach

The bottom-up approach, on the other hand, places a higher priority on departmental or divisional application of the model than on structure and application to the corporation as a whole. Therefore, the requirements of the part or segment supplant those of the whole corporate structure in the operation of the models. Information requirements are ordinarily established by the department or division for which the model is designed and constructed. Model users are likely to be operating managers and financial or operations research specialists, rather than corporate executives, although provision of guidelines or intervention by top management often occurs at an early stage of the model development.

One representative bottom-up model is Owens-Illinois's strategic system.[28] The desire to develop a computerized model to meet both the technical and format requirements of all divisions of the company was precluded because of its extreme size and complexity. Technical difficulties forced each division to develop its own model. It was consequently necessary to evaluate the overall program with a corporate model comparing common and special reports from the divisional models.

Brandt and Poszgai predict the expansion of the divisions' models as follows:

> The divisions' models varied greatly. The number of modules within a divi-

sion depended on the number of product lines handled as separate profit centers. As models are revised the trend will be to treat more product lines as profit centers.[28]

Another example is Telecommunications Earning Estimation Model (TEEM), developed for the security analysts of Wells Fargo Bank.[30] This model is reasonably sophisticated, probabilistic, and interactive. It is designed "to estimate an income statement and a balance sheet for any manufacturing or distribution corporation for which historic data is readily available."[31] The bottom-up approach is justified because this model is not intended for use by corporate executives nor division managers, but rather by financial analysts.

Even if the information flow from the model is bottom-up, the success of the model can be measured by the increase in communication both from top management to financial analysts and from financial analysts to top management. Many who advocate the initial construction of submodels[32] feel that complete corporate models, insofar as they are the ultimate objective, should employ the bottom-up approach. Some of the weaknesses of the bottom-up approach are summarized below:

1. Information requirements tend to be too detailed. (This does not necessarily means that the model is flexible.)
2. Coordination with other departments or divisions is ordinarily difficult, unless a very clear guideline is established at the preliminary or initial stage of the model development.
3. Flexibility in application and expansion to the higher echelon is less likely.

Eclectic Approach

The eclectic approach includes both the top-down and bottom-up approaches. While a corporate model is being built, an accounting-financing submodel or divisional models are separately constructed. Bottom-up and top-down approaches are coexistent.

The Burroughs Corporate Simulation Model,[33] Dayton Hudson Corporation Financial Planning Models,[34] and RCA Business Planning Model[35] are representative examples. Although the first two models provide divisions or operating companies as well as the corporate office with answers to "what if" questions, the RCA Business Planning Model serves only the information systems division. However, the conception of the RCA Business Planning Model began with top management initiatives for basic strategy evaluations and interaction among specialized technique-oriented models. Therefore, in the construction of the model, comprehensive corporate requirements and divisional requirements have been taken into consideration.

Some kind of eclectic approach is probably inevitable, since the top-down and bottom-up approaches alone have weaknesses. Through the appropriate introduction of the eclectic approach, the information requirements gap is alleviated, unnecessary details avoided, and allocation of human, material, and information resources is made more efficient.

USERS AND USES

Users of corporate models can be divided into three classes: corporate executives and divisional or departmental managers; specialists in planning, finance, and accounting; and students (potential executives, managers, or specialists).

Executives and Managers

Most users are executives or managers. For sound, progressive, feedforward[36] decision making, many models already have been constructed, utilized, and evaluated. Even if all users are executives or managers, however, their initiatives and participation take varied forms. Some are involved from the beginning to the end of model design, construction, utilization, and improvement. Others participate only at the preliminary or initial stages of model development. Still others do not participate at all, until they first use and ridicule the model.

It is important that users take initiatives at the important stages of model development. Accounts of successful model development have shown a close, direct relationship between success and participation and initiatives by users. For instance, as a result of active participation by top management in developing the "Banker" model, Lastavica says:

> Financial statement and time-sharing computer systems combined provide an extraordinary tool for top management. This tool has enabled our bank to have a better understanding of our present financial and marketing position and has enabled us to plan more definitely our corporate future.[37]

Such were also the benefits from top management participation in the development of FORPLANCON.[38]

Specialists

The second class of model users are varied specialists. Some corporate models are built to provide information to these specialists rather than to executives or managers. Organizations involved in consulting, software services, or managerial services often construct corporate models which are to be utilized by specialists rather than executives.

One of the typical corporate models used by specialists is the Telecommunications Earnings Estimation Model (TEEM)[38] as partially mentioned in the previous section. This model enables analysts to derive an earning estimate for a company through simulation.

> The model is probabilistic because estimates of financial variables are expressed in the form of probability distributions; it is interactive because *active participation by the Security Analyst is required* to operate the model; it is simulative because the analyst is allowed to change estimates entered into the system after he has observed and evaluated their impact upon other variables.[40]

The question arises as to how the analysts adjust system-generated estimates with their own estimates. The answer is as follows:

> ... the Analyst, not the model, is responsible for the accuracy of the estimate, and therefore, the Analyst must explicitly accept a system generated estimate, or replace it with one of his own. Thus, the system generated estimates are *advisory* to the Analyst—he is provided with the value of the estimate and a measure of the reliability of the estimate.[41]

The system-generated estimate is interpreted to be based on assumptions of normality.[42] Therefore, estimates derived by the analyst supersede the system estimates whenever an abnormal year is expected.

The assumption is that the analyst has access to causal variables exogenous to the model and can identify their effect on such endogenous variables as operational income, gross profit, etc. Thus, the analyst must know some of the contingency variables well before contingency action is taken. Realistically, it would be extremely difficult for the analyst to discover, supply, analyze, and report all pertinent information before the data requirements of the model are identified.

It is therefore important, first of all, that communications to and from an executive or an ultimate user of the model be substantial, even if the direct user is the analyst, and that effective input data organization systems and output data propagation systems be established.

Second, some sort of monitoring or appraisal system is required to follow up and continuously analyze the analyst-generated and system-generated estimates.[43]

And third, the user objectives should be explained in terms of the purpose of the output—it should be made clear what the user's specialty is, and in what form, that is, raw or analyzed, the output is expected.

Students

The third class of model users is composed of students, mainly potential executives, managers, or specialists, although in some cases the present executives, managers, or specialists are involved. The corporate model is therefore used for training or educational purposes. Numerous models have been established for business games[44] and decision simulation.[45]

Recently, there has been a tendency to make these educational models more sophisticated and wider in coverage in order to reflect a more realistic environment. It is important, however, that models used for the purpose of training, particularly elementary training, be fairly simple, so that students can comprehend the system within a short period of time.[46]

Ideally, various models should be available, in accordance with the educational objectives of each user. Sophistication should vary from teaching simple manipulations on terminals or posting figures into an input form, to long-term education in gaming and simulation.

To use corporate models, executives require training, and this should be carefully undertaken in order to prevent their untoward emotional responses. For example, in duscussing potential frustration and irritation, J. Harry Goldie, Corporate Director of Planning at The Boeing Company says:

> The next two irritations which diminish management confidence are possibly the most serious. My generation and those older than I are quite comfortable in our approach to problem solving. . . . When we attempt to use the new techniques that management scientists advocate, we suddenly find that we are out of the loop. A bright young man takes my problem away and translates it from managerese to computerese. Then he comes back with answers, so he tells me. Now any general manager worth his salt deals with "experts" in lots of fields about which he knows less than they do. He has learned sneaky ways of checking their work: penetrating questions, quick-and-dirty calculations, insistence on step-by-step tracing of the process, etc. We managers have trouble getting you guys to even talk to us. Talk about a generation gap. This is indeed an irritation. Another related irritation that I have is with the attitude that, because of this generation gap and language barrier, all of us "old timers" have to go to special classes and seminars to learn the new ways to get up to speed. I've got news for you. A lot of the old timers aren't going to go, for lots of reasons, some good and some bad; and for the most part, they are going to continue to be the boss for some time.[47]

INFORMATION REQUIREMENTS

If the most important information requirements can be identified, the chances of constructing a successful model are significantly improved. Because information requirements differ according to users it is always necessary to explore the information needs of each group of users of a model. Organizational hierarchy, differentiation of functions within an organization, and corresponding planning horizons are three main divisions according to which the information requirements of an organization may be discerned. It is imperative, therefore, to divide the combined requirements of users into information elements, according to logical categories for incorporation in the model.[48]

Writings of model users and builders have made it a relatively simple problem to ascertain the typical information requirements of models in general; however, it is ordinarily a painstaking process to identify the specific and essential requirements of each organization.

As Gaylord A. Freeman indicates,[49] one specific requirement may be confidential personnel information. In the case of INCO, specific forms separate from an ordinary financial statement were designed for one aspect of corporate planning and control.[50] The basic structures of some of these informational forms are shown in figures 2-1 through 2-4, which indicate forms other than an

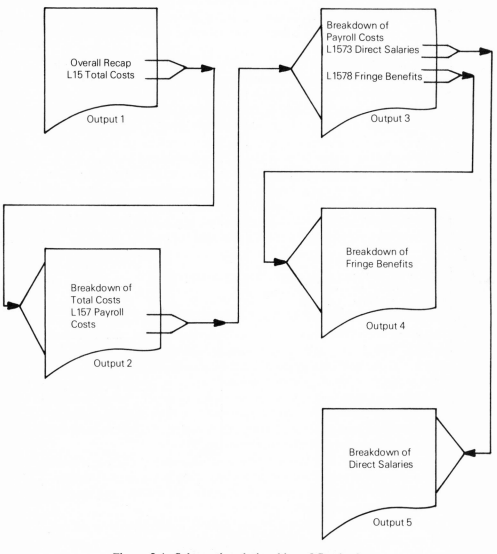

Figure 2.1. Schematic relationships of five basic
outputs —structural relationships of various costs.

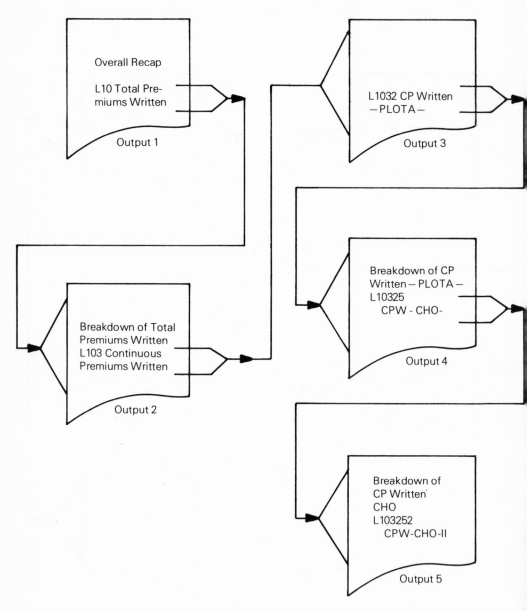

Overall Recap

L10 Total Pre-
miums Written

Output 1

L1032 CP Written
—PLOTA—

Output 3

Breakdown of Total
Premiums Written
L103 Continuous
Premiums Written

Output 2

Breakdown of CP
Written — PLOTA —
L10325
    CPW - CHO-

Output 4

Breakdown of
CP Written
CHO
L103252
    CPW-CHO-II

Output 5

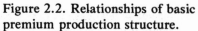

Figure 2.2. Relationships of basic
premium production structure.

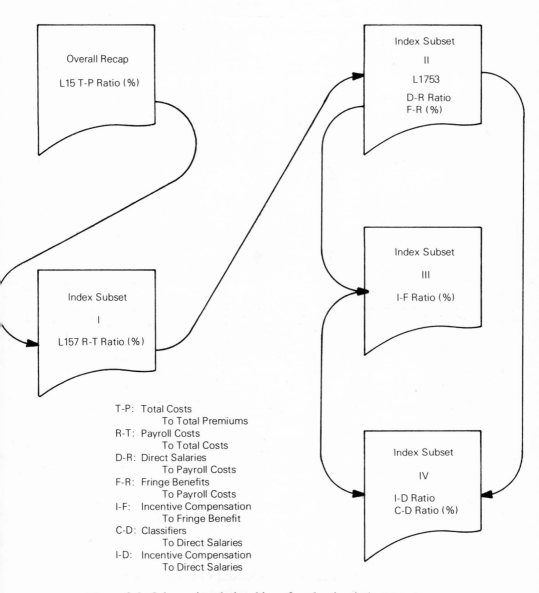

T-P: Total Costs
          To Total Premiums
R-T: Payroll Costs
          To Total Costs
D-R: Direct Salaries
          To Payroll Costs
F-R: Fringe Benefits
          To Payroll Costs
I-F: Incentive Compensation
          To Fringe Benefit
C-D: Classifiers
          To Direct Salaries
I-D: Incentive Compensation
          To Direct Salaries

Figure 2.3. Schematic relationships of evaluation index structure.

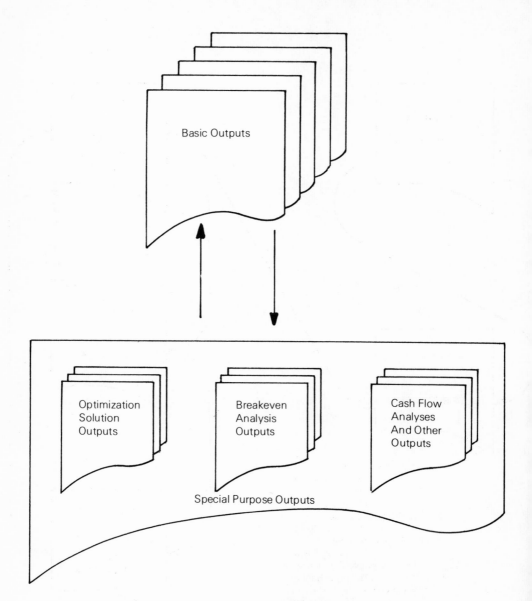

Figure 2.4. Schematic relationships between basic
outputs and special purpose outputs.

ordinary financial statement, and the analytical relationships among information elements.

Ackoff outlines the broadest general information requirements:

> ... information is required not only in order to become aware of the need to make a decision and to make it but also in order to evaluate the decision once it has been made and implemented.[51]

Different industries are finding it necessary to compile their own lists of specific financial data requirements. To establish sound nationwide financial planning and control, internally as well as externally, analysts are making their data requirements known on an industry-by-industry basis. The great diversity of individual American enterprises makes such an approach necessary. This expedient of analyzing competitive companies within the same industry or the whole industry is certainly less efficient than the first approach that hypothesizes peculiar information requirements for each company. For the purpose of determining specific information requirements, broad statements applicable to all companies may have little value. The general terms of both finance and accounting are asset, earning, liability, equity, and supplementary data adequately elucidating the economic and financial dynamics of the corporation. To this end, the exploration and identification of information requirements are undertaken according to a certain mixture of hardware and software systems. An example of such a mixture is Figure 2-5.

A trade-off analysis can reveal whether a new system should be installed or a present system can be used. If the present system is to be used, it may nevertheless be necessary to change the level of its objectives of hardware and software requirements. More detailed discussion in this regard follows in the next chapter.

DATA MANAGEMENT

Data management for the model encompasses many tasks, generally including at least data collection, data processing, data retrieval, and data utilization.

Data Collection

Data collection management entails collecting data that are quantitatively sufficient, qualitatively reliable, and helpful for decision making. To achieve the objective of data collection, each datum must meet these three data requirements.

Data are sufficient if they allow the model to function and produce meaningful results. In some cases, these outputs become new inputs to other models, in addition to separate raw data which are fed in at various stages. Therefore, data collected must cover the information required by the group of models, as indicated by Chambers, Mullick, and Smith.[52]

Data are reliable when free from bias or error, but maintaining and recognizing their reliability is very difficult. It is not uncommon for different sources to

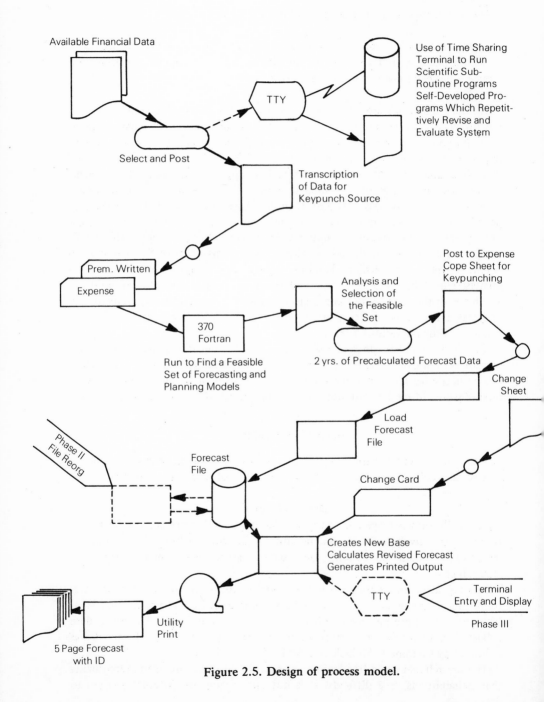

Figure 2.5. Design of process model.

generate different data from the same information.[53] In order for data to be workable, they should be collected according to the information requirements of the user.

Sufficient data do not mean too much data. In constructing corporate models, several builders have found the endeavor to acquire compendious data time-consuming but of little value. Examples of their reports follow:

... Initially we tried to include too much data in our model. Our modellers spent too much time on data rather than techniques.

... The extensive effort on data collection and updating data has diluted the efforts of our model builders.

... Contrary to what some people have indicated here, we have narrowed our scope of the type of input required instead of expanding it. We had too much detail in our initial determinations of cost ratios and performance indicators. We have continuously reduced the amount of data that has gone into the current version of our model.[54]

On the other hand, it is still difficult to gather enough relevant data.

Our principal limitation has been lack of adequate data.

We have had a limitation in terms of historical data in our data base. We had to gather much of our data manually.

... Our limitations are neither hardware nor software. They are the availability of information—historical information and the accessibility of current information.[55]

These comments of model builders reflect their experiences, and therefore have important implications that both model builders and users should keep in mind.

Data Processing

Data processing management embraces all management of data processing functions and systems related to computers and software systems. The key objectives of data processing management in the framework of corporate models are the following:

1. To generate the required outputs with utmost efficiency, that is, minimum turnaround time, and with the most appropriate computer programs.
2. To store the required inputs most efficiently, that is, using the best storage devices such as tapes, disks, drums, etc., appropriate to each system, with the most appropriate data base.
3. To update the data base frequently (permanent or temporary updating), and with the most effective methods, and to validate the updating.

4. To report the required outputs in the most effective manner,[56] that is, through printouts, display devices, or audio-visual devices, etc.

The model user should be cautioned that a model tends to generate an excessive amount of outputs. Kohlmeier[57] suggests, as a remedy, that routines to summarize, compare, and analyze the output of the model be included within the computer. However, the extensive analysis of information requirements and the delineation of options in summary form, intermediate form, or detailed form should prevent the generation of excessive information. Furthermore, output forms must be carefully structured according to the level of requirements.

When the timing phase is crucial for generating outputs, an on-line, real-time system is called for. For the users' purposes, this system could be had in interactive corporate model systems.[58] It is important for a user, in this case, to determine to what extent he needs output on a conversational basis. One simple solution is to order each output according to priority. If a cutoff point according to urgency is given, then for immediate purposes, outputs above the cut off point can be transferred to an on-line system. An entire transferring schedule from off-line to on-line can be established on the basis of careful and thorough studies. Subsequently, a change in programming language between the two systems may be required. Among various program languages, however, the use of Fortran is predominant; so far, Cobol, PL-1, and Dynamo have replaced it only among a very small percentage of users of time-sharing systems.[59]

Updating the data base generally has been a painful job for model builders. In order to facilitate this time-consuming and costly job, the data base should be made comparatively small and uncomplicated at the outset. If a large and sophisticated initial data base is inevitable, an automated data updating system should be designed and constructed in such a manner that it can be incorporated into the total model system. As indicated by System FP/70 in Bonner & Moore Associates,[60] for example, automated updating may be partially achieved, since the rest of the data is generated by the Perform Arithmetic procedure.

Regarding the importance of data base considerations, Summers says:

> It's probably true that a smaller number of people are involved in developing the data base, and the management of it can be less formal. I would think, then, that the data management function is somewhat like a gun. . . . The data management seems to have become more important, more time consuming and more costly than the model construction itself, and it involves not only gathering the data, but making sure that once it's produced it doesn't go into one of those hernia-producing files over there but is distributed out to the people who are going to use it.[61]

Data Retrieval[62]

Data retrieval management is in a broad sense one function of data generation management. The objective of data retrieval management is to enable a data user to acquire access to relevant data whenever required. Particular emphasis are, therefore, placed on on-line retrieval and well-ordered format of data, through which further analysis or retrieval can be easily performed.

It should be noted, however, that the data retrieval encompasses different connotations, depending upon the requirements of the information user, in a broad sense. It includes the retrieval of a string of symbols, of a datum or fact, such as a call number, of a set or sets of large symbol strings represented by a document (documents), and varied combinations aforementioned.

It is, therefore, clear that for the model system builder all the possible information requirements be preconceived and stored on the basis of (the historical) usage frequency and priority order so that successful retrieval can be accomplished within a short period of time. The model system user should bear in mind, on the other hand, the identification of information requirements by the builder has the builder's inherent limitations. It is desirable for the user to cooperate fully and provide the kind of information to be required in the future as systematically and clearly as possible in the earliest period of the model system design.

Data Utilization

Finally, data use management is a follow-up management of data generation. It entails ascertaining how effectively generated data are used. Since the findings of data use management become the basis of the improvement of the data generation system, the data use manager carefully analyzes not only the reference and use of the generated data but also evaluates their effectiveness or benefit.

The two objectives of data use management are: (1) to identify and order the value and importance of the generated data, while at the same time attempting to identify important data that has not been processed, and (2) to identify and order redundant and useless data, which might originally have been considered important.

Data use management is, therefore, a continuous process of discovering required data and eliminating unnecessary and outmoded data. Effective data use management can easily be attained through communication between model builders and users, on the one hand, and through an effective data use evaluation system on the other.

MANAGEMENT SCIENCE TECHNIQUES EMPLOYED

Management science techniques embrace all available scientific techniques for corporate operations planning, organization, and control. There are many bases of classifying these techniques. Among them are the processes of operations, functions, or activities common to various organizations,[63] and the problem-solving stage in all managerial activities.[64]

In his survey, Gershefski found the simulation to be the technique most commonly employed. He states:

Ninety-five percent of the models were of the case study, simulation type. Only five percent were mathematical programming, or optimization models. Eighty-eight percent of the models were deterministic in nature. Twelve percent were stochastic in nature, i.e., did consider a probability distribution for each of the key factors.[65]

Because of the difficulty in formulating certain analytic mathematical relationships, mathematical or optimization models are understandably less frequently utilized.

The problems inherent in simulation are its costliness and difficulty or verifying results. The following pertinent comments were made by Reitman, Ingerman, Katzke, Shapiro, Simon, and Smith:[66]

Simulation has a reputation for being one of the *most expensive* Operations Research techniques. Even though the cost reductions and increases in efficiency possible through simulation studies can be great, they are often indirectly achieved and not easily verifiable.

The high cost is usually offset by the benefit earned. Use of the model should increase total wealth by more than the cost of the model. However, it is not easy to quantity the benefits. Seeking a method of computing the value of the corporate model, Gershefski attempts to answer the following question: "Do formal planners exhibit a greater growth in net income and/or sales than informal planners?"[67] He supposes that "the value of the model is tied to the value of information and to the value of the planning process itself." In other words, identification and analysis of a certain case or event that is important needs to be explored.

In order to anwer this question, he defines two growth rates: the preplanning growth rate and the planning growth rate. The former is the rate of growth before the company begins formal planning, and the latter is the rate of growth after formal planning. Then, the planning effectiveness ratio (PER)[68] is computed for petroleum, chemical, and manufacturing industries. (Table 1.)

According to Table 1, for all the industries the Sales Planning Effectiveness Ratio and the Net Income Planning Effectiveness Ratio are higher with formal planning than with informal planning. In other words, formal planners exhibit a greater growth in net income for sales than informal planners. Gershefski warns, however, that these findings are based on a sample too small to be statistically meaningful, and advocates further research. Moreover, formal and informal planning should be defined more explicitly in terms of goal structure, planning and control mechanisms, etc.

Another approach to weighing the benefit is that of examing the case or event setting. For example, if management attempts to minimize total corporate costs while sustaining the levels of corporate productivity, and if a group of mathematical programmings is formulated for the purpose of generating alternative planning systems, then the result of the present planning system can be compared with those of these alternative systems. Should one alternative planning system reduce total cost compared to the present planning system, then the difference in the total benefit between the alternative planning system and the present planning system can be compared with the incremental cost (for this job) of the corporate models. If the difference is larger than the incremental cost, it is obvious that value be added by contributions of the model to the alternative planning system. More detailed discussions in this regard occur in Chapter V.

The problem of determing the validity of the results of simulations is subject to continuous discussion.[69] The approach most frequently taken is to compare the results with empirical knowledge. If the hypotheses are simplified and inputs are few, the comparison with empirical knowledge is easier. If communications between model builders and users are frequent, the probability of recognizing invalid output is largest. Lastavica says in this regard:

> You can test your answers against experience (by the use of time-sharing) very rapidly until, in a sense, you validate some answers and have a consensus. In this case, for example, if you were trying to make any changes in our planning model the first thing you would want to do would be to come up with a set of assumptions and find out what growth and earnings per share had been. You know what the model "predicts," and you also know what it's been historically. If the changes don't reproduce the past faithfully then you know some of your assumptions are out of line. You immediately start thinking what could be out of line.[70]

The weakness of this approach is, first of all, the unreliability of empirical knowledge. Second, because of the tendency to overvalue empirical knowledge, results that differ from the ones derived by educated guesses may be undervalued even though they must be true results. And finally, the simulation can easily serve the model users' personal interests rather than the corporate interests.

A comparative approach has been used in an attempt to surmount these weaknesses by checking the results of simulation with analytical results before human guesses intervene. To effect the check, a set of models is often utilized. For instance, in Shemer's discrete event simulation model,[71] two queuing type mathematical models supplement the simulation. The first of the mathematical models presents "worst case" estimates, whereas the second model provides "best case" estimates. If the simulation results fall between the upper and lower estimates, the probability of the validity of the simulation is increased. The limitation of this approach is that it requires that mathematical models be formulated. If mathematical models cannot be established, then this approach cannot be adopted.

Although the application of mathematical programming in optimization models is infrequent, according to Gershefski's survey its application to submodels is probable in the future. New management science techniques are also expected to appear as the development of corporate models is extended.

Table 1
THE RELATIONSHIP BETWEEN FORMAL
PLANNING AND FINANCIAL PERFORMANCE

	Sales Planning Effectiveness Ratio (PER)	Net Income Planning Effectiveness Ratio
Petroleum		
Formal Planners	8.7	10.31
Informal	8.1	3.30
Chemical		
Formal Planners	1.31	2.33
Informal	.85	.58
Manufacturing		
Formal Planners	1.28	1.51
Informal	.68	.82

Source: Schrieber [67], p. 36.

Note: Sales $PER_i =$

$$\left\{ \frac{\text{Sales Compound Growth Rate during the planning period}}{\text{Sales Compound Growth Rate during the preplanning period}} \right\}_i$$

Therefore, for formal planners,

$$\sum_{i=1}^{n} (\text{Sales PER})_{i/n} = \text{Sales Planning Effectiveness Ratio}$$

For instance, $\sum_{i=1}^{3} (\text{Sales PER})_{i/3} = 1.5 + 5.2 + 19.4 = 8.7$

The same approach is applied to Net Income PER.

CONCLUSION

In studying, evaluating, and developing models for planning and control, seven key elements of such models need to be given attention. These have been individually examined in considerable detail in this chapter.

There are, of course, many other considerations when the models are viewed from the perspectives of other characteristics, such as whether they are manual or computerized, on-line or off-line, interactive or noninteractive, monitorable, or nonmonitorable, probabilistic or deterministic, etc. These classes are frequently employed for technical purposes from the viewpoint of model builders. However, the considerations flowing from an examination of the seven characteristics enumerated are, in the author's opinion, the most basic to making sound developments and improvements in corporate models in the future.

SUPPLEMENTARY READINGS

1. Batt, Christopher D. et. al. Some Tentative Findings on Corporate Financial Simulation Models, *Operational Research Quarterly*, Vol. 25, No. 1, pp. 149-67.
2. Burch, John G., Jr., and Strater, Felix R., Jr. *Information Systems: Theory and Practice*. Santa Barbara, California: Hamilton Publishing Co., 1974.
3. Couger, Daniel J., and Knapp, Robert W., eds. *System Analysis Techniques*. New York: John Wiley & Sons, 1974.
4. Revsin, Lawrence. *Replacement Cost Accounting*. Englewood Cliffs, N.J.: Prentice-Hall, Inc., 1973.
5. Schussel, George. Business EDP Move to Data Bases. *Business Horizon*, December, 1972.

REVIEW QUESTIONS AND PROBLEMS

1. What do you think are the possible taxonomical schemes in classifying and evaluating the fundamental characteristics of corporate models?

2. What are the justifiable reasons why you have adopted the above taxonomical schemes?

3. How should the corporate models be designed and constructed to support the ultimate objective of a corporation (an organization)?

4. What agents would be necessary to analyze and elucidate a general objective into more specific objectives, so that corporate models contribute through these objectives?

5. What are the requirements of those objectives to be successfully incorporated into the corporate model?

6. Why and to what extent should corporate models be constructed?

7. What conclusions can be drawn from Gershefski's survey?

8. What should be the functional scope of a corporate model?

9. In order to define the scope of the model (and also corporate objectives), what must be obtained?

10. What operations can a corporate model be applied to? How can operations be classified?

11. How should we consider timing requirements inherent in a corporate model?

12. What are the design methods?

13. What design methods do you prefer? Indentify and discuss advantages and disadvantages of each design method?

14. Analyze and review three cases of the top-down approach.

15. Analyze and review three cases with respect to the bottom-up approach.

16. What eclectic approach do you suggest and why?

17. On the basis of two approaches, top-down and bottom-up, what should be the requirements for the eclectic approach?

18. What users are included in a corporate model?

19. How should the corporate model be tailored, depending on the class of users?

20. What considerations should be made to design and construct the corporate model behaviorally feasible?

21. What is the significance of identifying information requirements through the process of constructing and evaluating the corporate model?

22. In which ways are the information requirements better identified?

23. How can you draw the schematic relationships of information requirements?

24. Are the information requirements the same connotation as the outputs for a user?

25. What tasks are encompassed in data management for the corporate model?

26. What should be entailed in data collection management?

27. What does data processing management embrace?

28. What should be the essential objective of data retrieval management?

29. What are the two important objectives of data use management?

*30. Classify and discuss management science techniques to be employed in the process of design, construction, and evaluation of the corporate model.

31. What taxonomical basis for classifying management science techniques do you think best and why?

*32. What methods can be employed to validate the existing corporate model?

NOTES

1. For example, Gershefski [1], [2], Kohlmeier [3], Glans, Grad, Holstein, Meyers, and Schmidt [4], and Murray [5] follow similar taxonomical schemes and frames of reference. They are, however, either more specialized (concerned with a certain model) or too generalized. The author's knowledge of FORPLAN-CON and other models is used to identify and discuss the key characteristics.

2. This statement is on the basis of the author's experience.

3. This statement presupposes the "goal-orientedness" of aggregate human behavior.

4. See Gershefski [6] , pp. 26-42. Emphasis added. For additional surveys, see Dickson et. al. [47] and Grinyer and Batt [48] .

5. There exist numerous analyses of corporate objectives, especially profit maximization. The author identifies three main streams, classical (traditional) organization theory emphasizing scientific management, economic theory, and program budgeting, with regard to the sources of this relationship. For further details see, for instance, Kast and Rosenzweig [7] , pp. 57-139, Caplan [8] , pp. 7-46, and Ishikawa [9] , pp. 6-12.

6. Satisficing is a term coined by Simon [10] , pp. xxv-xxvi.

7. See Caplan, op. cit., pp. 28-30.

8. Application of models is considered to be for financial purposes when they are used to evaluate alternative operating or investment strategies, to provide revised financial projections rapidly, and to determine the need for long-term debt, etc.

9. Gershefski [2] , p. 42.

10. Glans, Grad, Holstein, Meyers, and Schmidt, op. cit., p. 18.

11. Ibid., p. 51.

12. Glans, Grad, Holstein, Meyers, and Schmidt, op. cit., pp. 51-53.

13. Ishikawa [11] , pp. 13-34.

14. Ibid., p. 4.

15. Further discussions with respect to the means and techniques of objectives improvement or refinement are in chapters IV and V.

16. Jaffe [12] , pp. 120-27, says that "in determining the system task requirements the system designer must ask and answer the following questions:

(a) What are the tasks?

(b) Why is each task performed?

(c) Where is each task performed, and where are the resources which are manipulated?

(d) By whom or what is each task performed?

(e) With what is each task performed?

(f) When is each task performed—that is, under what conditions, at what times? In short, what happens to initiate, continue, terminate, or reiterate the task performance?

(g) How is each task performed?

See also Shaw and Atkins [13] , pp. 109-10.

17. For details, see Abe [14] , pp. 82-83. For example, region is divided into sixteen areas, such as Japan, Philippines, Hong Kong, Viet Nam, Thailand, etc. Each area has several categories, i.e., Esso Sekiyu, Plaza Trading, and Tonen. Each category subsumes business lines.

18. See Brown [15] , p. 113.

19. See Ishikawa [11] , p. 6.

20. Chambers, Mullick, and Smith [16] , p. 159.

21. Fraser [17] , p. 361.

22. Ibid., pp. 361-62.

23. The New York Life Corporate Model has been in use since 1970. In the spring of each year, the model is run for twenty years using a set of "standard" assumptions. Eighteen to twenty alternative runs are then made to compare with the standard. Basic assumptions as to interest rates and investment turn over are supplied by their Investment Department; inflation rates are supplied by their Economic Department; and sales assumptions are supplied by their Marketing Department. The remainder of the input data is developed in the Actuarial Department. The Model has been quite successful and has met wide acceptance. They have found, however, that their model is input bound. Because of the large amount of input data required, it takes them a good three months to produce a final standard run. It is their plan to have a tool to produce projections at a much faster rate. They are considering the development of a new model which would produce 90 percent of their current output with possibly a 50 percent reduction in input.

24. Freeman [18] says, "We chief executives not only want the information immediately available, but we also want it confidential and available to no one else. . . . There are many times when I don't want anybody else to know what I am thinking about in connection with our people."

25. Ayers, Kroeger, and Moseley [19], p. 2.

26. Lastavica [20], p. 2. Emphasis added.

27. This statement becomes more valid in cases where a model is to be used particularly for internal control purposes.

28. For details, see Brandt and Poszgai [21], pp. 1-6.

29. Ibid.

30. Wagner, Akutagawa, and Cunco [22], pp. 396-430. This model is no longer employed at Wells Fargo Bank. During the last three years (1972-1975), corporate modeling done by Wells Fargo Bank has been aimed at answering particular, one-shot questions posed by senior management, e.g., simulation models to evaluate loan growth strategies, holding company acquisitions, and short-term borrowing strategies. However, recent concern for long-term planning of the Bank's asset/liability structure has necessitated development of a corporate model to analyze more completely the input of alternative strategies. At this point in time it could be characterized as a top-down, deterministic model for senior management.

31. Ibid., p. 396.

32. The reasons why submodels should be established at first are many. However, they may be divided into two categories. One is based on the assumption that the corporate model is an idealistic concept and that it is impossible to construct it from a technical point of view. For instance, see Dyment's remarks [23], p. 4, "There is a strong temptation to try to develop a 'total' corporate computer model, complete with automatic sales forecasting, inventory-level optimization, and even production scheduling and machine loading. In more than one instance, such programs have become so complicated that they are unworkable." The other reason for not attempting to first formulate a total corporate model stems from the assumption that the corporate model is not

idealistic, but essentially unattainable, because of the difficulty of identifying information requirements. See, for example, Schrieber [24], p. 8.

33. Pryor [25], p. 60, and Khoury and Nelson [26], pp. 13-21, indicate some of the differences in inquiries between the division level and the corporate level as follows:

At the division level:

1. To learn the combined influence of independent decisions.

2. To improve decision-making ability (a) to enforce discipline through formal relationships; (b) to allow the testing of independent decisions; (c) to point out problem areas; (d) to point out some inconsistent areas in decision making.

3. To allow divisions to make several test runs before preparing their detailed forecasts.

At the corporate level:

1. To learn the effect on the corporation of a proposed divisional plan.

2. To evaluate divisional "profit plans" and study alternative plans with respect to (a) growth objectives; (b) asset management; (c) profit maximization; (d) cash flow.

3. To evaluate corporate decision alternatives.

4. To prepare long-range financial and debt management plans.

34. See Smith [27], pp. 1-3.

35. See Robuck [28], pp. 1-13.

36. As to the application of the feedforward concept, see Ishikawa and Smith [29] and Ishikawa and Smith [30]. Two of the examples concerning the application of feedforward concepts is seen in the corporate models at American Airlines and Campbell Taggart, Inc. For details, see Struve [31] and Campbell Taggart's case, *Business Week*, December 7, 1974, pp. 72-78.

37. Lastavica, op. cit., p. 194. For Bank Planning Models, see Ishikawa, Carson, Eames, and Huang [51].

38. In the case of FORPLANCON, top management had had previous experience in model development, and were therefore able to provide timely guidance. For more details, see Ishikawa, op. cit., p. 40.

39. See Wagner, Akutagawa, Cuneo, op. cit.

40. Ibid. Emphasis added.

41. Ibid., p. 401.

42. The term normality here connotes that "everything goes on as is assumed to be without being disturbed by unforeseen factors." See Ibid., p. 401.

43. Wagner, Akutagawa, and Cuneo, op. cit., p. 401, underscore the necessity of an "open structure" in the internal design of the model to optimum analysis and evaluation. Their aim is at combining system estimates whenever a new verification technique is developed for all or some subset of the companies.

44. There are numerous writings concerning business games. Three representative items, which cover wide aspects of models and their history as a means of college education, are Kibbec, Craft, and Nanus [32], Graham and Gray [33], and Cohen, Dill, Kuehn, and Winters [34].

45. In most cases, "decision-simulation models" means the same as "business games" or "management games." If the managerial decision-making aspect of a model is more emphasized than the gaming aspect, the term "decision-simulation model" is frequently used.

46. See Rehg [35], p. 532.

47. Goldie [36], p. 20.

48. If the required information can be categorized into a certain number of classes in a logical manner, then a kind of tree structure or cascading system will be established, as indicated in the Corporate Model System of the Standard Oil Company (N.J.). See Abe, op. cit., pp. 82-83.

49. See Freeman, op. cit.

50. Ishikawa [11], p. 40.

51. Ackoff [37], p. 99.

52. Chambers et al., op. cit., p. 159.

53. See, for example, Ishikawa [11], pp. 37-39.

54. Doenges, Summers, and Tavis [38], p. 99.

55. Ibid.

56. The priorities and preciseness of the information outputs should be given specific attention.

57. Kohlmeier, op. cit., p. 6.

58. Interactive corporate model systems denote a group of corporate sub-models that can function interdependently or independently in an interactive manner by the use of time-sharing systems.

59. Schrieber, op. cit., p. 42.

60. For details, see Bonner & Moore Associates, Inc. [29], pp. 1-9.

61. Doenges, Summers, and Travis, op. cit., pp. 69-70.

62. For data retrieval in general, see, for example, Meadow [52]. GENIE (General Information Extractor) by APL Services, Inc. is an example of an English-language data base reporting and retrieval system for time-oriented data on an interactive basis.

63. For instance, one can classify operations research or management science models on the basis of common processes, such as communication, control, decision, financial, forecasting, information, inventory, production, marketing, scheduling, service, simulation, testing, etc.; see *International Abstracts in Operations Research*, published by the International Federation of Operations Research Societies.

64. As to the classification, see Ishikawa [9], [40], [41], [42], [43], [44].

65. Gershefski [6], p. 41.

66. Reitman, Ingerman, Katzke, Shapiro, Simon, and Smith [45], p. 261.

67. Schrieber, op. cit., p. 34.

68. See the note in Table 1.

69. See, for example, Naylor and Finger [49] on the issue of verifying computer simulation models and Ignall, Kolesar, and Walker [50] on empirical validation of the analytical models.

70. Doenges, Summers, and Tavis, op. cit., p. 65.

71. For details, see Shemer [46], pp. 282-89.

CHAPTER III

Developing A Corporate Model[1]

INTRODUCTION

The experience of developing various computerized models showed that the practicality of a model can be diminished if the development process is not given careful attention. A study of experiences of other model builders has also contributed to this conclusion as to the importance of the development process.

This chapter identifies the key considerations and sequence of developmental activity in constructing corporate models. It should contribute, therefore, to a better understanding of the types of activities that are necessary for those who contemplate the construction of a successful corporate model.

KEY CONSIDERATIONS

The three key considerations for developing the corporate model are (1) the exchanging of information through questionnaires, (2) adjustments required by corporate policy changes during model development, and (3) thorough coordination among model users, model builders, and their mediators, if any. These considerations are essential in planning, organizing, and controlling the development of the corporate model.

The Exchange of Information Through Questionnaires
Generalization to Specification. Doenges regards the problems of introducing a corporate model as being no different from those associated with the introduction of any new tool. He says:

> . . . during the introductory stage, there are tool makers and tool uers. If you can get both together, you are in good shape, if you can't you have problems. A lot of the usage problems. . . , both on the surface and below the surface, relate to the problems of getting tool users to talk to the tool

makers, of getting both groups to communicate and associate with each other.[2]

The need for communication between model developers and users persists from the beginning of development to the final use of the model. And, it is important that it be the right information at the right place at the right time, conveyed with the right means.

Since the information requirements of the user may be uncertain at the initial stages of development, especially when the model is directed at corporate headquarters problems, a need will probably arise for a mediator who can communicate sympathetically with both model users and builders. The mediator should be able to understand the major problems and requirements of both groups, and thereby facilitate the exchange of vital information. One promising technique that the mediator can use to foster the necessary, continuous, and systematic exchange of information is through the use of questionnaires.

In establishing FORPLANCON, ten questionnaires were issued by the author and answered within a short period. Most of them attempted to identify and define objectives, scope, users, and related matters. For instance, one questionnaire was designed to determine the weighting factors for each accounting item in a time series basis. From the answers it was possible: (1) to determine the number of years for the time series as a whole, that is, past and future years; (2) to determine the number of past years to be considered for purposes of forecasting a specific number of years into the future; and (3) to assess the reliability and consistency of each datum from previous years.

Respondents' answers to this questionnaire were fairly similar, and therefore the weighted average method was adopted as the basis for obtaining forecast figures.[3]

Although, as Prince[4] indicates, there are other means, the questionnaire-response system produces the following benefits:

1. Investigation of key characteristics and requirements can be systematic. Therefore it can be determined when a past, present, or future endeavor to identify the key characteristics and requirements was, is, or will be effective.

2. Any change in a user's requirements during model development can be anticipated from the outset of model development. Because information collected through questionnaires can be systematically organized, illogical or sudden changes in information requirements during development (which could make the model redundant or ineffective) are unlikely.

3. Differences of opinion among model users can be resolved as they are revealed by their answers to the questionnaires. Hence, the need to incorporate contradictory requirements from different users of the same model is reduced. (The organization of users in model development is discussed later in this chapter.)

4. Priorities can be identified according to the degree of detail and order apparent in the answers to the questionnaire.

Identification of Priorities. To describe categories[5] of information or jobs is not to establish their relative priorities. Priorities are usually determined on the basis of corporate strategy (long-term planning) or on the basis of operational control (short-term planning). When the value judgments of users are significantly different, it is difficult to establish even minor priorities. Furthermore, it is often impossible to correct the model for changes in priorities because of excessive time lags in identifying them. Townsend states:

> NICB[6] publishes all sorts of data about corporate practices. I have found it a valuable source for ideas—on what not to do. When the vast majority of big companies are in agreement on some practice or policy, you can be fairly certain that it is out of date.[7]

Therefore, perceptive model builders avoid incorporating outmoded priorities by including certain highly probable alternative priorities. The model must then take into consideration corporate traditions, societal values, the influence of specific managers, and the informal goals of the organization.

Pressuring model users to identify and communicate timely priorities to model builders may often be necessary to enable model builders to be of service in the future. Practically, determination of priorities is not a discrete job, but a continuous one, since priorities are established in planning and development as well as decision-making processes. The establishment of priorities in planning and development determines the procedural order of model development. The establishment of priorities in decision-making processes can be mapped into a selection or job priority matrix[8] or decision tree.[9] Both are identified on the basis of answers to questionnaires.

The crucial differences between a job priority matrix and a decision tree can be summarized as follows:

1. A job priority matrix stipulates in matrix form the procedural priorities in information processing by determining the relative values of the types of financial information sought. On the other hand, a decision tree predicts in tree form the probability of a decision being made and its probable results.
2. A job priority matrix is a means of information processing. A decision tree is a means of decision analysis.
3. A job priority matrix is mainly deterministic. A decision tree is mainly stochastic.

It is necessary to establish efficient criteria and techniques for ascertaining relative priorities of steps in developing corporate models. Some concepts and techniques that have been found meaningful are further discussed in Chapter V.

Extent of the Examination. To determine how flexible a model must be, numerous hypothetical questions must be asked. As different versions of the questions are asked,[10] additional solutions may be revealed. Questions asked explore: (1) functional relationships; (2) acceptable deviation from original predictions; and (3) recourse if deviation is more than is feasible with the model.

The hypothetical questions for which the model must account cover certain independent and dependent variables.[11] It is sometimes very difficult to ascertain functional relationships reliably enough to meet the user's precise requirements. To the extent that the functional relationships disclosed in answering the aforementioned questions are deemed accurate, the output derived from these functional relationships may be deemed reliable. In practice, the veracity of all descriptions of functional relationships must be checked, as the use of falsely and/or inaccurately described relationships could produce unrealistic results.

As the model becomes more complicated, there is a greater need to ascertain the extent to which a dependent variable or a set of dependent variables deviated from the standard prediction[12] in the past. If the functional relationships are nonlinear, this need increases because the domain of reliability is more restricted, even if precision increases for a narrowed area.

In cases where it becomes necessary to make decisions beyond the capacity of the model, it is necessary to prepare another model or another set of models, so that at least some reliability of the whole model is maintained. If this is impossible, the limitations of the model and the approach to overcome these limitations must be defined.

Future Development and Expansion of the Model. It is natural that the efficiency of the model will be improved over time. Subsequent modification or expansion of a model is often impossible, and in most cases this is due to the lack of insight by either the model user, model builder, or their coordinating agent during the original process of model development. A basic guideline during model building is that the model should be built in such a way as to permit expansion in the future, even if the required time for building a certain unit of the submodel is extremely short.

Future development and expansion can be prepared for through stage-by-stage and package concepts. The former is the stipulation of an attainable goal of the model and the stages by which it will be attained. One example is shown in Figure 3.1. At a minimum, user, objective, scope, and the detailed features of the software and hardware should be described on a stage-by-stage basis.[13]

In the case of the package assembly approach,[14] (see Figure 3.1) basic package determination is very important. The package unit is frequently a basic financial model for a certain operation. Because this basic financial model has applicability to other operations, corresponding parametric changes of financial information are necessary. Important factors such as user, objective, and detailed features of software and hardware arrangements are usually stipulated in the same context, and are thus not changeable as in the stage-by-stage approach.[15] The advantage of this approach is ease in assembling one package with another. However, the disadvantages include difficulty in identifying basic packages, and inability to include certain information to a particular package independent from another.

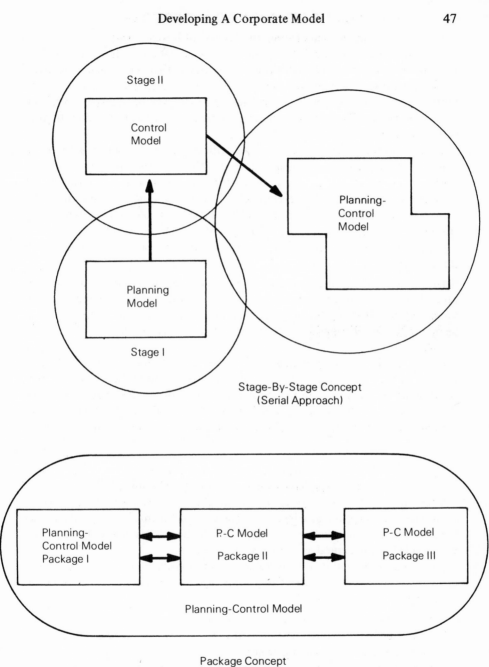

Stage-By-Stage Concept
(Serial Approach)

Package Concept
(Parallel Approach)

Figure 3.1. Two main approaches for model
development and expansion.

Adjustments During the Process of Development

If in the process of model development a basic corporate policy changes—that is, centralization to decentralization or diversification, etc.—then objectives, scope and other aspects of the model also have to be altered. It is not easy to keep abreast of all changes,[16] but because it might even be necessary to recommence modeling efforts, it is desirable to anticipate the necessary alterations as early as possible.

Some probable policy changes can be anticipated at the outset of development, or at least during preliminary analysis. The need to anticipate changes as early as possible is particularly important with respect to policy changes that alter the priorities of model development. In such cases the relationships among various models which could tolerate such alterations should be fully explored at the outset. In addition, when a steering committee[17] represents the user, it is necessary to ascertain whether or not the committee has fully considered the policy change.

Timely adjustment of the model to meet policy changes can only be achieved through adequate anticipation by the task force for modeling development. And the ability to anticipate future policy changes is dependent upon the task force being continuously supplied in formation that will assist prediction of policy changes.

General guidelines for avoiding unnecessary delays caused by policy changes include: (a) continuous investigation of the environmental factors which may cause some policy change in the organization; (b) continuous understanding of the key issues in the company which may affect modeling development; and (c) continuous communication with an authoritative member of the user group.

Coordination[18] of the Activities of Key Users, Model Builders, and Other Personnel

Literature on the subject of coordination often ignores the important matter of human coordination problems in system development.[19] Successful model building requires thorough coordination of all the parties involved. Generally, this entails both structural and process coordination.

Structural coordination usually relies on the organizational hierarchy, and in connection herewith understanding and agreement need to be obtained regarding:

a. Identification of the ultimate user or group of users.
b. Identification of those who are to have *authority* and *responsibility* for evaluating and the modeling project.
c. Identification of those who can assign the *necessary personnel* under a given procedure.

Once those essential matters have been taken care of, and a task force for the modeling project has been formed, decisions must be made as to:

a. How often participating persons or groups should meet.

b. The extent to which basic understanding and agreement must be obtained at each meeting.

c. Alternative coordination procedures, that is, a direct coordination with model users without passing through the task force, etc.

Once basic understanding and agreement regarding the frequency of meetings, alternative coordination procedures, etc., are obtained, process coordination is required. Process coordination involves dynamic coordination on a time-phase basis. In process coordination, attention is directed to matters such as:

a. The appropriate time for terminating the proposal of a general framework (see discussion below) and the enumeration of problems should be established.

b. The appropriate time for culminating the preliminary analysis.

c. The appropriate time for involving a computer scientist or programmer in the project and the extent of such involvement.

d. The types of model (deterministic or stochastic, discrete or continuous) that should be established.

e. The specific computers and auxiliary equipment required for the model and how often, etc.

Hence, process coordination is follow-up coordination. It is concerned with discovering successive applications of available procedures, operations, and resources. Emphasis is on continuous adjustment of information and timetables, even if structural coordination has been accomplished at the initial stage of model development. Structural coordination, in contrast, is required at the initial stage and at "milestone checkup points."[20]

Practically, therefore, structural and process coordination can often be made simultaneously, although this often depends on the relative emphasis on structural versus process coordination.

It is extremely difficult to develop and maintain coordination. Although some coordination is mandatory at the pre-established milestone points, the need remains for an integration of process (continuous) coordination efforts into a feasible, workable model in the long run because of changing sets of requirements.

ORDER OF DEVELOPMENT

On the basis of the author's experience, the following seven steps have been identified as indispensable stages in the development of a corporate model:

1. Proposal of a general framework reflecting some felt-need problems of groups of users.

2. Preliminary analysis for the proposal.

3. Identification of information requirements.

4. Design and construction of the hardware-software (model) system.

5. Test of the constructed model.

6. Application of the model.

7. Revision or expansion of the model.

These actions may not occur in exactly the stated order. In some cases, for example, while design and construction of the hardware-software system is in progress, some new felt-need problems may be presented by the model user. This then dictates a need for revision of the model. Likewise, during application of the model, new information requirements may be identified. In such cases, corrective action must be consistent with the established development process or operation procedures.

Proposal of a General Framework Reflecting Some Felt-Need Problem of Users

The initial conception of the modeling project is usually a function of the background, experience, and enthusiasm of the user, and the extent to which the management of the organization deems the project necessary. Note the following observation:

> Three years ago our chief financial officer said, "[We] should have a corporate planning model." When he was asked what the model should do, in other words, how he wanted to use the model, he said, "I don't know, but other companies are beginning to build models so we'd better do it, too."[21]

In INCO's case, the modeling project began with no rigid requirements and goals, but rather from a discussion of the most desirable steps for developing the model within a certain operation. Its purpose was to assess the importance of this operation (a continuous policy operation) in relation to all combined company operations. Therefore, at the outset, considerable time was spent identifying the operation in all the functions, that is, accounting, marketing, production, research and development, etc., in the corporation.

When a detailed framework of requirements has already been determined, this stage can be excluded. Development can therefore commence with preliminary analysis or identification of information requirements. The requirement that a general framework first be established forces the model builder to find out how the modeling problem occurred. It is quite likely that this investigation will draw attention to the concerns and needs of people inside and outside the organization. He should then be able to more accurately compare alternatives, and therefore generate a more efficient proposal. Major defects of including the general framework as a specific step, on the other hand, include the possibility of consuming too much time before proceeding to other stages. Furthermore, there is the chance that a significant modeling problem may be obscured as a result of time devoted to reaching agreement on the extent to which human, material, and monetary resources should be employed. This problem can be overcome by strong leadership on the part of a particular user or group of users.[22]

Preliminary Analysis

Although some authors have tried to distinguish preliminary analysis from feasibility assessment or analysis[23] on the basis of the degree of formality or the difference in objectives, the preliminary analysis seldom precludes some degree of feasibility assessment.

The preliminary analysis must at least determine the objectives of the model (from the user's expression of needs), alternative approaches to attain these objectives, and the necessary personnel, material, money, time, and information requirements. Although information requirements of the user are not definite at this stage, some possibilities can be anticipated on the basis of discovering the fundamental activities or essential relationships within the institution.

Moreover, the anticipated benefits of the model must also be clarified at this stage. Because a decision maker compares required resources with anticipated benefits, it is necessary to show him as specifically as possible what savings or benefits can be expected from the model in dollar terms or some comparative efficiency index. If the evaluation of benefits is difficult, as is frequently the case, they can be expressed in ranges, rather than single figures. Evaluation in terms of ranges is often more realistic, and may generate more confidence on the part of top management.

Identification of Information Requirements

If the preliminary analysis is approved by the users or their appointed steering committee, then the next necessary step is the determination of information requirements. These information requirements should be initially identified by users and builders when proposing evaluation of the feasibility of developing new corporate model systems. Detailed requirements, however, ordinarly cannot be specified in the early stages.

Procedures for identifying information requirements must vary, since requirements vary with users. Felf, for instance, demonstrates the extreme demands of the management of his company as follows:

... one of the reports that management was using was a report about this wide ... say 24 to 30 inches. It was a 12-months projection. The question was: "Can you reproduce this report?" Well as you all know, the computer has certain limitations, and one of the things it cannot do is to produce a report that is 24 inches wide. Well, we spent approximately ten or fifteen minutes discussing how we would reproduce this report by printing three reports together. We didn't laugh; we took this very seriously, this was what management wanted to see, and if anything was going to be done, it was going to be done in management's terms.[24]

Another model builder describes the problems encountered when the information is required in the same form as in regular accounting control reports:

We have found that management will not use the model output unless it is very detailed, and in fact in the same form as the regular accounting reports which they get for control of current activities. But my problem is that I can't report back to management in that level of detail on the results because their data assumptions are not that detailed.[25]

In the two aforementioned cases, the model builders tried to meet fairly specific information requirements. And the findings were that it is impractical to construct a model in the absence of such specific requirements. For example, Collier writes:

We tried to get them [management] involved from the beginning. We weren't always very successful at that, consequently we, as a matter of necessity, built this model pretty much by ourselves. But we won't do it again. In other words, if management is not willing to be involved to the point of telling you specifically what they want, then they don't need the model and won't use a model if they have one.[26]

In constructing INCO's model, the model builders continuously solicited specific information requirements through both general and specific questionnaires and supplementary interviews. The model builder and user must identify the information requirements at the level of detail mutually agreed upon no matter how difficult it may be.[27] Although some authors contend that a decision maker's information preferences cannot be obtained,[28] at least some information about his preferences is readily available;

1. Corporate policies reflect the decision maker's preference. It is possible to analyze and evaluate corporate policies if necessary.
2. Many companies employ "management by objectives," "management by systems," and "formal planning,"[29] which may reflect the decision maker's preference.
3. Some decision makers do try to make their preferences known.

Inherent in the decision maker's authority, moreover, is the responsibility to guide his subordinates in management by elucidating his preferences as far as possible.

Design and Construction of the Hardware-Software System

Since the information requirements dictate the combination of hardware and software systems, the design and construction of these systems proceeds in two directions. One is the development of the most workable mathematical or process model (software system), and the other is the development of a well-balanced, economical hardware model which can accommodate the software or process requirements.

It is at this stage that "overall quality" is built into the model. Subsequent performance of the model will reflect this quality, and the extent of coordination among users and builders, that is, accountants, financial analysts, specialists, system engineers, and programmers.

Because of the importance of the software system, and because of the degree to which an existing hardware system tends to dictate the design of a software system, the latter should, ideally, be independently designed and constructed. This would mean that the hardware system should be constructed or applied to accommodate the requirements of software systems. In practice, however, it is very inefficient (because of time and cost requirements) to design software systems independently. If this independence of design cannot be achieved, then, at a minimum, the model designer must be apprised of the state of the available hardware system.

If the firm does not have an installed hardware system, it must first ascertain the availability of appropriate hardware systems. A trade-off analysis of whether a new system should be installed or the present manual system used should be made as early as possible. If an existing manual system or relatively unsophisticated computer system is to be used, there may be a need to adjust the objectives or system (hardware, software) requirements of the model.

Consequently, there are many engineering and economic problems to be solved at this stage as well as the next stage.[30]

Test Run—Hypothetical Situation

The results of a test run frequently reveal poorly organized or weak links in the model. Although it is generally considered time-consuming to select a wide range of parameters for examination in a test run, such a run is important. The main foci of debugging are on errors relating to the fundamental functional characteristics (for example, linear vs. nonlinear) of the model itself, and on input or programming errors.[31]

Supplementary well-programmed error diagnostic routines facilitate error detection and in the long run can save substantial time. The model is programmed to include a diagnostic routine which reveals the effectiveness of the system, and it is therefore not difficult to decide whether or not sophisticated diagnostic routines are economically feasible.

With FORPLANCON, at least eleven diagnostic routines were introduced. These included a format detection routine, limit, coefficient, and reassignment file diagnostic routines,[32] and an equation selection table diagnostic routine. The number and quality of the routines enabled the researcher to detect input, programming, etc., errors in the model and ascertain whether the model would generate unrealistic results. In this way these routines helped to validate the effectiveness of the model. Careful evaluation of the test run also aided in confirming the flexibility or limitations of the model. For example, it often happens that the computerized model includes more complex assumptions than can be handled in a manual planning and control model. This in turn leads to an inability to validate the results of the computerized corporate model, and therefore a need to change the number and complexity of the input assumptions. Numerous test runs are thus required.

Application of the Model

Once the test run has been successfully completed the model may be applied to real situations. The user must have easy access (it must be readily available to the model). He requires sufficient instruction (availability of instruction manual and oral instruction) to familiarize him with the model. Thereafter, it is the author's experience that the user may well work with the model for periods longer than planned. The user thus trains himself to generate the most meaningful results. He is able to do this because of his ability to control the inputs.

Obviously, the model must meet the requirements of the user, preferably beyond original expectation. Since applications frequently require augmentation of the model, which often becomes the basis of future expansion, it is valuable to use the constructed model as often as possible.[33]

The results of the application of the model can usually be evaluated on the basis of certain criteria.[34] One of the most important criteria is the extent to which the results represent the real situation. In a model such as FOR-PLANCON, which began as a method of short-term forecasting, the figures forecasted by the model were compared with those forecasted by division managers as well as with the actual figures.

A second evaluation criterion is the ability of the model to tolerate new and successive changes of the variables. New figures which appear after each simulation run need to be compared with those generated by the user's forecasts, educated guesses, etc.

A third evaluation criterion is the application potential of the model. Since, in most cases, the direction of expansion is suggested in the preliminary analysis, the model is simply examined to confirm some previous evaluation of a need for revision or extension of the model.

Ultimately, of course, the acceleration of modeling development is usually dependent on successive application and evaluation of the model.

Revision or Expansion of the Model

It is useful to the overall modeling development program to describe each simple unit model, since each model is interrelated. Therefore, the completion of one unit model may entail the design and construction of another model to which it is most directly related. Alternatively, it may entail the improvement or expansion of a previous unit model.

In the case of FORPLANCON, three alternative approaches to expansion and revision were proposed, and the advantages and disadvantages of each approach summarized and compared. The first alternative was a steady expansion of the scope of application of the original model based upon successive appraisals by model users of FORPLANCON. This approach requires: (a) deletion, replacement, or addition of various variables; (b) change of more than two variables at the same time; and (c) Application of the model to other operations such as marketing, claims, and data processing, etc. The second alternative was to improve (including expansion) the corporate financial model on a corporate rather than a divisional basis. Thus, the model would cover overall corporate requirements rather than simply summarize each division's figures. And the third alternative was to decentralize various functional areas of the model. This approach leads to clarifying more detailed functional characteristics in a systematic manner.

The first alternative basically involves an improvement and sequenced expansion of the applicability of the model. One model builder describes such an approach to expansion as follows:

Although our model is basically an accounting model, we are going to expand our model into manpower and facility requirement projections. These two things can be derived directly from the financial-type data that is in an accounting-type model.[35]

Another model builder says:

The next major development will be optimization. In the long range I plan to work on alternative generators. The third one would be more development in behavioral modeling in order to input forecasts consistent with the plans. The fourth one would be the extension of an aspect of modeling which we have not talked about at all: modeling as an aid of decision making. . . . Finally, I would like to see the production of what I call learning models. We are perhaps five or six years away from this. But in anything we do there are certain patterned answers; we should study this pattern in initiating each new planning cycle.[36]

With reference to the second alternative, the following discussion by another model builder in connection with on-line real-time computer system models is relevant:

Future activities will be in the direction of on-line real-time communication with the computer system models providing direct output and more emphasis on the economic environment in which we are working.[37]

A model builder for the Xerox Corporation illustrates an approach to revision where revision involves the replacement of an old model with a new one. This approach is relevant to the third alternative.

We have a number of models which are supplanting XPM [Xerox Planning Model]. The emphasis in the future will probably be on decentralization of the various functional areas of the model and development of the impact of the functional areas in more detail on a simpler basis.[38]

Most model builders expect their models to be increasingly decentralized from now on. They believe that decentralization may enable the corporate staff to offer useful advice on how to build models at the various division levels so that these models may be compatible.

CONCLUSION

In order to develop a corporate model, the sequence of developmental activity must be understood. The examination of various corporate models, including FORPLANCON, shows that the builder must be constantly aware of each of the key considerations and of the stage of development, but he must also maintain the perspective of the whole process. The valuable experiences of various model builders and users—some time-consuming, of little value, and avoidable—show the importance of identifying in advance of construction what is required of the model. Requirements of the model must also be examined incessantly in the sequence of each developmental activity. Saving of time and cost can thus be achieved, particularly in cases where substantial change of requirements is inevitable.

Finally, revision or expansion of the model can be approached from a number of perspectives, depending on the purposes of the revisions. Three alternatives, that is, a gradual expansion and improvement, discrete expansion onto a corporate basis, and decentralization, are worth the attention of both the model user and the model builder.

SUPPLEMENTARY READINGS

1. Kelly, Joseph F. *Computerized Management Information Systems*. New York: The Macmillan Co., 1970.
2. Lucas, Henry C., Jr. *Computer Based Information Systems in Organizations*. Chicago: Science Research Associates, Inc., 1973.
3. Shubik, Martin, and Brewer, Garry D. "Reviews of Selected Books and Articles on Gaming and Simulation," Rand Corporation, R-732-ARPA, June, 1972.
4. Tenneco, Inc. Case in *Corporate Planning Models*. Austin: Graduate School of Business, The University of Texas, 1971.
5. Trent, Robert H., and Wheelen, Thomas L. *Developments in Management Information Systems*. Encino, California: Dickenson Publishing Co., Inc., 1974.

REVIEW QUESTIONS AND PROBLEMS

1. What are the three key considerations for developing a computer-based corporate (organizational) model?

2. What should be the prime considerations in exchanging information through questionnaires;

3. What role should a mediator play in the process of identifying information requirements of the model user?

4. What benefits do exist when you employ a questionnaire-response system? What does Prince say as to the benefits of the questionnaire-response system?

5. How are priorities of information requirements usually determined?

6. What considerations should be made in addition to incorporating certain highly probable alternative priorities?

7. What do you think is the best approach to identify and communicate timely priorities to model builders?

8. What are the differences between a job priority matrix and a decision tree?

9. To determine how flexible a model can be, what hypothetical questions must be asked?

10. Delineate your corrective action in cases where it becomes necessary to make decisions beyond the capacity of the model?

11. What should be a basic guideline during model building?

12. What representative concepts do you advocate for the future development and expansion of the model?

13. Discuss advantages and disadvantages of the concepts you advocate for the future development and expansion of the model.

14. Depict the concepts and approaches you highlight comparatively.

15. If in the process of model development a basic corporate policy changes, what would you do as a person responsible for model construction?

16. What should be of incessant concern to you as a model builder and model user when probable policy changes can be anticipated at the outset of model development?

17. What are the general guidelines for avoiding unnecessary delays caused by policy changes?

18. How do you classify coordination of activities of key users, model builders, and other personnel in model development?

19. How do you define structural coordination?

20. How do you define process coordination?

21. Discuss basic differences between structural coordination and process coordination?

22. Describe the steps indispensable in the development of a corporate model.

23. Discuss how each step does relate the next step or other steps. Depict these relationships as lucidly as possible.

24. What at least should preliminary analysis encompass?

25. Do you think that at least some information about your model user's preferences should be readily available?

26. What should be the prime consideration in designing and constructing a hardware-software system?

27. What are the representative techniques for debugging a program?

28. In what way do you attempt to validate the constructed model?

29. Discuss some validation approaches you know to validate the computerized corporate model.

30. Summarize important considerations with respect to test running of the model.

31. What is the prime consideration in applying the model succeeding to test run?

32. On what criteria is the computerized model often evaluated?

33. What alternatives do you think you bear in mind in revising and expanding the model?

34. How can you try to maintain the perspective of the whole process while constantly being aware of each of the key considerations and of the stage of development?

35. How can you try to maintain the perspective of the whole process while constantly being aware of each of the key considerations and of the stage of development?

36. Summarize the key considerations in each step as well as from the perspective of the whole process.

37. Relate the result in the above question with the persons concerned.

38. Relate the result in the above question with the possible techniques to be applied.

39. Relate the result in the above question with the case where you are required to establish a computer-based organizational (public) planning and control model.

*40. Relate the result in the above question with the criteria of evaluation for the established model. How should the criteria be differentiated between the corporate and noncorporate planning and control model?

NOTES

1. This chapter is a revised version of Chapter III in Ishikawa [1].

2. Doenges, Summers, and Tavis, op. cit., p. 42.

3. Of course, there is no guarantee which method is best for purposes of forecasting. Such considerations as how many past years are considered in deciding the future, what emphases are placed on data for each year, and how the emphases are differentiated among categories of information are also important in using a questionnaire approach. The response of the questionnaire is further examined by means of observations and interviews.

4. Prince, on the basis of his own experience and that of other model builders, introduces a checklist as the first step in the process of specifying information requirements. See Prince [2], pp. 21-24.

5. For instance, Dearden, McFarlan, and Zani [3], p. 4, postulate five important dichotomies of business information:

(1) Action and nonaction

(2) Recurring and nonrecurring

(3) Documentary and nondocumentary

(4) Internal and external

(5) Historical and future

They say that "it is possible with this classification to divide all business information into 32 categories which can be useful in analysis of the information requirements of a business."

6. A few titles from the 1969 index of NICB publications will give you the idea:

a) "The Board Chairman—Positions and duties. A job description is included." From this came the conviction that job descriptions are absurd for jobs above $150 a week.

b) "Human Relations—Personnel directors' responsibility for employee motivation. . . . 'Employee Motivation—What role for personnel?' " From this came the conviction that we do not need a personnel department at all.

c) "Committees—Use of committees in developing policies. From this came the conviction that you should liquidate all permanent committees.

d) "Executives—Fringe benefits. Special fringe benefits, such as country-club memberships and chauffeurs to attract and hold top executives." From this came the conviction that you should not have any of this nonsense paid for by the company.

7. Townsend [4] , p. 20.

8. A selection (job) priority matrix is defined as a matrix which indicates specific priority requirements of each information element or financial item. It is, therefore, a representation of a user's decision mechanism (including his preferences), and all conceivable functional relationships among dependent and independent variables identified. For further treatment and discussion, see Chapter V.

9. A decision tree or a decision-flow diagram is defined as a tree structure and process composed of both decisions and outcomes that may be subject to change, as is seen in most of the literature related to systems analysis and decision analysis. For instance, see Hare [5] , pp. 38-42, and Raiffa [6] .

10. Many writers claim one of the main functions of the corporate model to be the "answering" of "what if" questions. For example, see Pryor [7] , Rappaport [8] , and Greenberg [9] .

11. The terms "explanatory factor," "input," "x variates," or "predictor variates" frequently denote independent variables, and the terms "predicted response," "output," "Y variates," or "criterion variates" correspondingly denote dependent variables. See Jensen [10] , p. 2.

12. The standard prediction for a company is the one derived by a method it has used for a long time—ordinarily its traditional forecasting techniques.

13. The stage-by-stage concept implies the intention to build mutually independent subsystems one by one and to connect them appropriately to create an integrated whole system. Therefore, one module does not necessarily coincide with one subsystem or sub-subsystem. "Module" is a constant in corresponding measurements. This means that the basis for measuring each module is the same

structurally or procedurally. Structural consistency is demonstrated in using the same hierarchical model with corresponding endogenous and exogenous variables, whereas procedural consistency is illustrated by using the same looping or iteration approach. The representative stage-by-stage approach is shown in Fraser [11], Des Jardins and Lee [12], and Struve [13].

14. The package assembly approach can be described as the module assembly approach. Some of the models which have adopted this approach are described by Chervany, Strom, and Boehlke [14], and Boulden [15], and Ishikawa [16].

15. A model builder for American Airlines writes: "At American Airlines we are attempting to blend an operating projection model and a financial projection model. We used two models that were developed independently in the industry. Now we are trying to make one talk to the other in a realistic manner. I think if we did it again we would develop a single model ourselves" (Doenges, Summers, and Tavis, op. cit., p. 97.)

16. Model Builders at the Corporate Planning Models Conferences, held at the University of Texas Graduate School of Business Administration, November 24-25, 1969, frequently made the following statement: "We would design for flexibility. We found that as our planning process changed, as it should, it was difficult to keep abreast of these changes." See Doenges, Summers and Tavis, op. cit., p. 98.

17. A steering committee is a supervising committee of the users' representatives. In many cases, a vice-president for operation or system development is chairman of the committee. For more details of the steering committee, see Blumenthal [17], pp. 123-32, and Gershefski [18], p. 68.

18. There are numerous writings on coordination. For instance, March and Simon [19] refer to "coordination by plan" and "coordination by mutual adjustment." These are related to process coordination. Thompson [20], Boulding [21], and Barnard [22], on the other hand, discuss coordination by emphasizing standardization, hierarchical structure, and interdependence. These are the concern of structural coordination.

19. Head [23], pp. 121-44, draws attention to this problem.

20. One of the milestone approaches is discussed by Stephen Enke, ed. [24], pp. 218-19.

21. Doenges, Summers, and Tavis, op. cit., p. 6.

22. A good illustration is seen in Dow Chemical Company's case [25], p. 17. The chairman took an initiative by asking a model builder key questions, e.g., "what would happen if our growth rates in loans were 'x' percent lower than they actually were for the last quarter?"

23. For example, see Sherman C. Blumenthal, op. cit., pp. 115-20.

24. See Doenges, Summers, and Tavis, op. cit., p. 30.

25. Ibid., p. 59.

26. Ibid., p. 18.

27. Burch and Strater [35] introduce five methods to identify specific information requirements.

28. Schrieber, op. cit., p. 8.

29. See Humble [26], [27] for "Management by Objectives," Neuschel [28] and Stokes [29] for "Management by System," and Gershefski [30], pp. 34-36, for "formal planning."

30. Two representative works on the economic and engineering analysis of computer systems and on time-shared computer systems are Sharpe [31] and Scherr [32]. A number of these problems will be discussed separately.

31. *Encyclopedia Dictionary of Systems and Procedures* [33], pp. 175-76, suggests several techniques for debugging a program, such as break-pointing, tracing, memory dumps, and printout of intermediate answers, and also describes three main causes of errors as (1) input errors in the tapes or punched cards that are used; (2) coding errors, such as using an incorrect address; and (3) logic errors, or using incorrect methods for solving a particular problem.

32. Limit files establish the +/− ranges of change in independent variables. Coefficient files enable a change in an independent variable to be translated into appropriate changes in dependent variables. Reassignment files enable crossfooting when there is a difference between a total arrived at by an independent calculation and the sum of subsidiary values making up the total.

33. On the other hand, Hibbs [34] advocates that model users and builders "be concerned about needed information being received by the proper people." He further says: "The top-level manager who concerns himself too much with the nitty-gritty details internal to the company may well become a victim of 'management myopia.' In fact, it has been suggested that the new information systems technology may aggravate this danger since executives may be encouraged to trust the system to provide all the information they need. For instance, in his book 'Practice of Management,' Peter Drucker cites the disaster of Ford's Edsel automobile. All the quantifiable evidence that could be produced showed that the lead balloon would fly."

34. The criteria discussed here are those used by the author in his research.

35. Doenges, Summers, and Tavis, op. cit., p. 102.

36. Ibid., p. 103.

37. Ibid., p. 104.

38. Ibid.

CHAPTER IV

Benefits From Computerized Corporate Models
and Ways of Acquiring Them[1]

INTRODUCTION

The objective of this chapter is to clarify exactly what model users, particularly, corporate executives can expect from computer based corporate models, and to outline specific considerations for ensuring acquisition of such benefits. The main reason for this discussion is that considerable misunderstanding exists as to what a model can do for a company. And many executives are unaware of the problems involved in the process of securing these benefits.

Before the executive requests a model builder to design and construct a model to assist him in planning, organizing, and controlling the operations he is responsible for, the executive should recognize just what kind of help the corporate model can provide his company. Often, his expectations are inconsistent with the capabilities of a model; consequently, his subsequent evaluation of its performance often reflects disappointment.

The model user must be aware of the economic and technological constraints on the model, but this should not prevent him from making seemingly impossible requests. The builder's creativity needs to be stimulated, and the significant requirement would simply be to clarify the relative importance and urgency of each of his requests.

With respect to the demands that are identified as being beyond the capability of the model, the executive must decide whether to request the model builder to develop methods of meeting these demands or to seek assistance elsewhere, for example, an outside consulting firm. Thus, the executive must define and evaluate each of his demands upon the model. The builder can meet the executive's requirements satisfactorily only if they are clearly stated in the order of their priorities.

Of course, if the executive believes that relaxing certain of his unattainable requirements does not seriously diminish the value of the overall potential of the model, then he might consider dropping them. Technological and economic problems are largely correlative to the sophistication of the executive's demands.

In the process of identifying the specific requirements, an executive needs to realize that a corporate model can provide two key services to a company. It can supply information basic to planning, organizing, and control. It can also supply information to improving the existing systems of the company.

CONTRIBUTION TO PLANNING-ORGANIZING-CONTROL[2]

Corporations follow a "management cycle" which involves such functions as planning, organizing, directing, coordinating, and control. In a large corporation, where management responsibilities are apportioned among divisions, success depends on the smooth functioning of the cycle to maintain efficient relationships among the corporate components. Even routine operations between headquarters and divisions require coordination and control.

Annual financial planning and control is one of the recurring activities involving various levels of organizational components[3] to which management might profitably apply a corporate model. For example, FORPLANCON was used by a large corporation during the October-December period when the annual financial planning guidelines were given to division managers. Each division manager developed his annual plan on the basis of these general guidelines.

A corporate manager must have some basis for evaluating material differences between the figures of the corporate guideline and those of division managers. Ordinarily, discussion starts from the previous year's variance between actual and planned figures. Both the corporate and division managers exhibit the results of a certain type of variance analysis, from which they try to develop a common interpretation of each variance. However, it is sometimes difficult to identify the reasons for certain variances, thus decreasing the ability of corporate management to take corrective action.

The goals of the corporation as a whole guide division managers' actions. However, if the establishment of multiple goals is inevitable, then several bases of control are necessary. For example, the outputs of FORPLANCON have contributed substantially to guidance and control in the following ways:

1. It reveals the reliability of a predicted set of figures in terms of an error rate or standard error of estimate.[4] A responsible manager can therefore make more confident judgments concerning the proposals of each division manager.
2. The model is easy to use, and a responsible manager can run simulations on the basis of the various assumptions of each division manager.
3. The corporate manager is able to observe the reliability of the prediction after six months' use of the model.[5] He is consequently able to examine more alternatives than before, to identify the factors which contribute most, and evaluate the soundness of planning.

4. Without FORPLANCON, a division manager's proposals may be accepted without adequate analysis. FORPLANCON permits additional analysis (via simulations by the Corporate Manager), and thus a more appropriate plan results. This in turn tends to narrow the gap between the planned and actual figures of a particular division.

The above four features can be described as reliability, useability, predictability, and suggestibility. These will be further discussed below.

The Reliability of a Predicted Set of Figures

To evaluate a predicted set of figures for planning, indicators of their credibility must be established. These indicators can produce an ordinal scale (for example, credible, less credible, and not credible) based on the standard error of estimate, F value, or residual values, or an interval scale where predicted figures cover a range, rather than a point based (for example, on standard deviation).

Each predicted figure is therefore collated with the corresponding indicator. The difference in the figures or ranges is then compared to the range of difference subjectively acceptable to the model user. If the allowable range is smaller than the range computed on certain criteria, then the prediction is questionable. Otherwise, it is used in the decision-making process.

The allowable difference between the predicted figure and the indicator is usually determined by the significance of the figure. The probability figure (α) that decision makers are willing to accept in assuming the deviations between actual and expected values is due to assignable causes (which may or may not be controllable), when in fact they may attribute it to nonassignable causes.[6] Although the α is frequently set at 0.01 and 0.05, determination of the significance of a planning figure is theoretically a complex process. Labovitz indicates six criteria for determining statistical significance:

1. Practical consequences of both the Type 1 error (rejecting a true null hypothesis) and Type II error (failing to reject a false null hypothesis).
2. Plausibility of alternative rationales and empirical evidence.
3. Power and robustness of the test.
4. Sample size.
5. Degree of control in design.
6. Whether the research objective is to test or develop hypotheses.[7]

Moreover, evaluation of the figure requires that the entire data management process and the validity of the techniques which produced the estimates and actual figures be examined carefully.

Certain questions must be asked in evaluating the data management process.

1. *Have all pertinent data been collected so that reliable estimates may be generated from them through a certain technique or set of techniques?*

Most literature concerned with the application of management science techniques assumes the validity and relevance of the data to be used. Practically, however, when it is found that there are weaknesses in the data collection system, it is not appropriate to use the data to generate estimates. This is especially true as a firm changes in structure and management methods. For instance, at INCO, operations have changed from semicontinuous to continuous. This has resulted from the fact that the process of establishing operational policy has changed from discrete to semicontinuous, and because accounting methods have changed from a cash to an accrual basis. The net result has been that many of their data have lost utility. If the same data collection system had been maintained, it would have been almost impossible to obtain raw data appropriate for purposes of generating estimates, that is, without substantially adjusting some of the data. The model builder needs to decide whether to revise the generated data or to change the data collection and generation system itself. He must therefore make a thorough review of the data collection and generation system. Three considerations are crucial to his decision.

(a) The required extent of revision and improvement of data (in terms of the revising process and the amount of revision).
(b) The timing and resource requirements.
(c) The assumed extent of change in data requirements in the foreseeable future.

2. *Have all data been processed so that each datum can be assigned an appropriate place for further processing or be given to a decision maker as an end product?*

In the framework of the planning-organizing-control process, required data is classified by its functions; planning data, organizing data, and control data.[8] It is essential that model builders identify the kind of data processing to be done according to the category of the required data. If a model user is well acquainted with the three categories, he can always pursue the best data-processing system in terms of the most efficacious use of the hardware system and generated data.

One approach to obtaining an efficient data processing system is to reorganize all data or software formats according to the three functional categories and attempt to eliminate repetition of the data or formats among the categories. Often a certain control datum can be obtained by a simple derivation from a planning datum.

3. *Have all the data been exhibited in a manner that maintains the distinction between actual figures and predicted figures?*

Some common ways to distinguish actual figures from forecasted figures in visual presentations are the use of different typefaces, different coloring, and the use of dotted lines or brackets to indicate predicted figures.[9] The method used is selected according to lucidity, and on the basis of convenience to the compiler and the typesetter.[10] Each presented figure can be best understood if appropriately presented with adequate supplementary information. Devices are thus adapted to human convenience.

It is also necessary to distinguish forecasted figures from planned (goal) figures. Although planned figures are speculative, they are treated as if they were actual or attained figures. Generally, forecasted figures are the primary figures by which planned, secondary figures are determined. Even a primitive type of

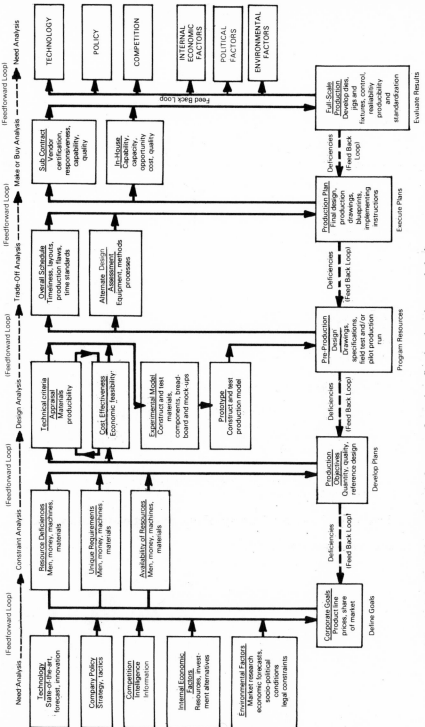

Figure 4.1. Graphic portrayal of a manufacturing firm's planning and design process.

Source: Bright [9], p. 170.

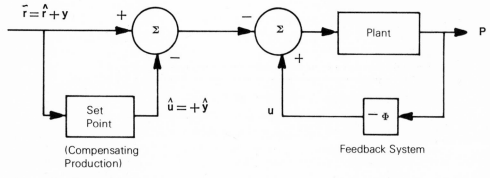

$\tilde{r}$ (t): Rate of Demand
$\hat{r}$ (t): An Unbiased Demand Forecast
r (t): The Respective Forecasting Error

It is assumed that (after some finite transient period) it will be possible
to arrange a mean product on such that

$$\hat{u} \ (t) = \hat{r} (t)$$

Φ: Linear Time Independent Control Operator
u (t): Linear Control Policies

Figure 4.2. Feedforward and feedback system in production-inventory model.*

*Source: Schneeweiss [14], p. 475.

corporate model (which offers only very basic forecast figures) should eventually generate predictions readily adaptable to dynamic planning.

Useability of the Model

Timely, economical generation of sufficient alternatives is required of the model. Model users must know that the capacity of the model is limited by the intelligence and technical skill of its builders. Timely generation of enough alternatives for planners with the least amount of information therefore requires that model users discuss with model builders qualitative differences of alternatives. Model builders should, in turn, inform users of the hypotheses and possible limitations of the model regarding these alternatives. Such dialog can be aided by the construction of conversational graphic systems.[11] Desmonde says:

> It would appear that in our creative thinking we often feel forced to objectify our thought processes in visual form. This enables us to examine our ideas in a more detached, critical, and objective way. A prime exemplar of this activity is the artist, who develops his themes through images. The creative technologist performs somewhat similar behavior with pencil and paper, which he uses to sketch possible designs or interrelations which are forming within his mind. Graphic systems can thus function both as scratch pads and as analytical assistants to the scientist and engineer.[12]

The use of a light pen to generate the number of alternatives through the conversational mode is, when fruitful, more convenient than using only a display terminal. Only recently, however, have conversational graphic systems entered widespread use.[13] As far as software is concerned, there are "few graphics-oriented operating systems in existence which are capable of handling multiple displays and a variety of input devices in a truly general manner."[14] Hantman describes two of the main barriers to the successful growth of these systems. One is the lack of easy-to-use, standardized "languages" for communication within the system, and the other is the increasing need for economic justification of the research.[15] The growth rate of these systems is constrained by the research and development cost to each company, as well as to a country as a whole.

Predictability

The predictability of information depends on the model user's understanding of what information requirements are predictable, what information requirements are less predictable, or least predictable—and why?

To increase the predictability of an area of concern, Bright suggests that four policies are mandatory in technological forecasting that are probably most difficult:[16]

1. A forecast should not be a one-time event, but should be continually revised as time brings technical, economic, and social horizons closer.
2. A policy of detecting errors and making incremental corrections should be followed in order to improve the understanding of relationships.

3. There should be a continual search for key factors that change or are sensitive.

4. The organization's own pattern of experiences should be considered and applied. This means that the firm needs data files on its own technological-economic history. Unhappily, very few firms maintain such files; and they have only folklore to use as a guide to plan future technical progress.[17]

Of the four policies, the establishment by the company of proper data files on its own technological-economic history is the most difficult, although there have been some rigorous studies to date. These studies hold valuable lessons for those who design and construct data files. With respect to the data file problem, Isenson reaches five conclusions:[18]

1. Real needs result in accelerated technological growth. In the absence of such needs, technological growth is inhibited.

2. The rate of growth of technical knowledge is directly related to the rate of change in the number of stable, better-educated scientists and engineers in technical areas.

3. For relatively well-established technologies, a constant rate of growth in relevant knowledge results in a decreasing rate of growth in technological capacity.

4. The rate of growth of knowledge is directly related to the relative level of informal, person-to-person communications in the relevant technical areas.

5. Advancing technology is made up of a number of precursor events and a far greater number of pedestrian accomplishments. The direction of technological growth can be inferred from the former, but the rate of growth will be dictated by the latter.

Both model users and builders must take the above factors into consideration when designing and constructing corporate models. Moreover, in assessing the predictability of various technological forecasting models, such studies as those of Jantsch[19] are of great help (particularly to model builders) in identifying and applying some of the potential techniques to a real problem.

Still another method of increasing predictability is for model users to have model builders examine the empirical, functional relationships important to decision making.[20] If careful investigation reveals empirical, functional relationships to be invalid, the data which produced the evaluation and the functional relationships in question must be re-examined. This approach is applied not only to technological forecasting, but also to any other kind of forecasting.

Techniques of prediction must also be investigated when the corporation formulates and executes a corporate planning and control system. For instance, if a manufacturing firm has a planning and control process as depicted in Figure 4.1, and if appropriate submodels for need analysis, constraint analysis, design analysis, trade-off analysis, and make or buy analysis have already been established, then each feedback loop would disclose the extent to which predictions had been realized, and therefore the extent to which goals were predictable. As suggested by Shneeweiss,[21] in the framework of a production-inventory model,

Table 1. How to Measure Each Criterion

Criteria	How to Measure
Predictability	Error Rate (i.e., (Actual Figure—Forecast Firgure)/Actual Figure) or Theil's Inequality Coefficient,* etc.
Reliability	Secondary Error Rate (i.e., (Actual Figure—Planned Figure)** /Actual Figure) or Inequality Coefficient, etc.
Useability	Number and quality of timely and economical generation of relevant alternatives (e.g., (Number of Alternatives—No. of Alternatives Used for Decision Making)/ Number of Alternatives, etc.)
Suggestibility	Number and quality of additional analysis (or findings) previously unexpected (e.g., maximize sales volume sustaining the presently available sales force → minimize total costs keeping the present sales volume, etc.)

*Theil's inequality coefficient provides an index that measures the extent to which a simulation model affords retrospective forecasts F_i of observed historical data O_i:

$$\text{Inequality Coefficient} = \left[\frac{1}{n}\Sigma(F_i-O_i)^2\right]^{1/2} \bigg/ \left[\left(\frac{1}{n}\Sigma F_i{}^2\right)^{1/2} + \left(\frac{1}{n}\Sigma O_i{}^2\right)^{1/2}\right]$$

For more details, see Theil (17, 18). In addition, predictability can be examined by various statistical tests, including the Chi-square Test, the Kolmogorow-Smirnov Test, and nonparametric tests, etc. For nonparametric tests, see Siegel(19) and Walsh(20).

**Planned figure connotes a more intelligently processed figure, as a result of additional factors being considered and analyzed in comparison to a forecast figure.

predictability can be examined by dividing the system into two subsystems: a feedback planning and control system and a feedforward planning and control system (Figure 4.2).

Suggestibility

The extent to which the information a model provides suggests still more information than the user expects and measures the extent of suggestibility in the application of the model. It is valuable for providing more qualitative information than expected for allowing productive inferences from the unforeseen information. Suggestibility, therefore, can be considered a bonus from the use of the model.

For example, a user seeking to maximize production within certain limited human resources might be interested in the result of minimizing labor costs while maintaining a certain level of production. (If a duality theorem is applied, the user can compute a second result easily.) If he finds that he can fruitfully apply the incidental result, his optimization model is considered *suggestive*. How to measure each criterion as to predictability, reliability, useability, and suggestibility is summarized in Table 1.

GENERAL IMPROVEMENT OF EXISTING SYSTEMS

The development of a new model frequently dictates the need to change the old system. At a minimum, the comparisons resulting from the development usually identify some inefficient aspects of the old system.

When INCO installed FORPLANCON, inconsistencies in the data reduction system were revealed, and a few approaches to overcoming the problem were proposed. Also, the correlation between change in a unit of information and the foundation and method of measurement became clear. For example, when the number of employees required for a certain division was disclosed, it was possible to obtain other relevant information as follows:

1. Whether or not it was the number of employees as of December 31, 1970, or,
2. whether or not that number was obtained by computing (the number of employees [NE] as of November 30, 1970) + (NE as of December 31, 1970 – NE as of November 30, 1970) X (yearly averaged turnover ratio excluding temporary employees), or,
3. whether or not it was the number of employees obtained by (NE, November 30, 1970) + (NE, December 31, 1970 – NE, November 30, 1970) X (six months' average turnover ratio excluding temporary employees), or,
4. whether or not it was the number of employees obtained by (NE, November 30, 1970) + (NE, December 31, 1970 – NE, November 30, 1970) X (six months' moving average turnover ratio excluding temporary employees), or,
5. whether or not it was the number of employees obtained by (NE, November

30, 1970) + (NE, December 31, 1970 – NE, November 30, 1970) X (three months' average turnover ratio excluding temporary employees).

It was also possible to consider the number of employees on the basis of a three months' moving average turnover ratio including temporary employees. If temporary employees are considered, various methods to count them would be required, and therefore the inconsistency of resultant accounting information would be inevitable.

Consistent relevance is maintained if the objective of each report dictates the exact definition of the variables included therein, for example, the "number of employees." The total reporting system can thus be examined and revised to assure that each processed unit of information meets the objective of each individual reporting system as well as of the total reporting system.

Approaches to improving existing systems vary. However, they can usually be classified as continuous or discontinuous. A continuous approach attempts to improve or expand present systems without substantially changing (for modeling purposes) their basic objectives, system configurations, and related resources. Continuous approaches avoid as far as possible increasing CPU time, storage capacity, or programming time, etc. It is, therefore, most efficient for model users to follow this approach, insofar as their information requirements can be satisfied by minor alterations of a present system.

If, however, fundamental change is required by additional information requirements, then a discontinuous approach is necessary. Such an approach differs from the continuous one only in the extent to which improvement of a present system requires changing its basic objectives, system configuration, or related resources. Such an approach necessitates careful system implementation planning, particularly with respect to the question of whether the necessary change affects (1) software systems only, (2) hardware systems only, or (3) both software and hardware systems. For example, if the model user needs to employ only one or two computer terminals which can be connected with an in-house central computer, his approach is continuous. However, if he must use a dozen terminals connected to a distant outside central computer with varied jobs to be processed, then his approach is discontinuous.

If the company has to develop many of its own modeling programs, then its implementation planning must take both software and hardware problems into consideration.

Change to a Time-Sharing System[22]

Should a corporation require extensive new or modified modeling programs, it must compare the costs and results of selecting a remote time-sharing system with those of continued use of the in-house batch processing systems already available. Therefore, in considering the time-sharing system the organization should determine whether or not purchasing or leasing the time-sharing system is more cost-effective than using present computer systems. The analysis should include this possibility and the possible benefits of developing an in-house time-sharing system.

One of the crucial problems that results from a continuation of use of an evolving, non-time-sharing computer system is ordinarily attributable to its off-line nature, that is, a time lag between the occurrence of a problem and the receipt of a solution, which impedes the use and effectiveness of a certain model or a software system.

If the company attempts to use a corporate model that requires a substantial amount of inputs, the following five factors must be considered to reduce the amount of inputs:

1. Transferring data from master-sheets to worksheets.
2. Transferring data from worksheets to coding sheets.
3. Keypunching.
4. Computer runs using a certain package.
5. Time lags between each job.

Each job takes a certain amount of time, $T_1, T_2, .., T_5$. Generally stated, the more inputs, the more time is required for $T_1, .., T_4$. The time lags depend on the efficiency of each job or work station. Moreover, since keypunched cards must be fed into a computer, two time lags are inevitable. One is the time lag between the completion of keypunching and feeding into the computer; the other is the time lag between the outset of the feed-in and the receipt of the output. The former time lag is generally larger than the latter. If the computer is scheduled to process uninterruptedly a number of jobs, the former time lag would be still larger, even if a well-designed multiprogramming scheme is used.

In developing a corporate model to be incorporated into a larger system, one ordinarily needs to feed in different kinds of inputs, particularly in the test run and evaluation of the model. Possible priorities for the use of the computer should therefore be explored fully so that probable queuing time may be ascertained.

The five factors identified above are all important in the consideration of time lag problems. However, if a time-sharing system is to be utilized, at least a substantial portion of the last factor can be ignored. Furthermore, the queuing time of the time-sharing terminal is generally negligible in comparison with that of a present computer system, even if in some cases the waiting rime from the key-in to response is fairly high. The large number of inputs to the terminal can be remedied by using paper tape, which minimizes the computer hook-up time, although the initial set-up time (for preparing the paper tape input) may be high.

Time-Sharing Systems vs. Present Systems

The main consideration in determining whether or not to add a time-sharing terminal is the benefit of timing relative to total costs in introducing a time-sharing system. For instance, if corporate simulation models are to be developed and solved, the best of the alternative methods must be found—for example, continuing the present manual system, using the off-line, in-house computer system, or leasing a new time-sharing system. Even in using an off-line computer system, some time can be saved through the use of a preprogrammed scientific package. This is also true in using the time-sharing system. Suppose that at least 500 regression equations need to be established. Even the construction of simple regression equations (if it were to be done manually) would require many manhours. Junior mathematicians or statisticians would then need to be hired (unless assistance by other departments or sections can be anticipated). The number to be hired would depend upon the urgency.

Thus, the relative benefits of the time-sharing and present system are computed by deducting manhours required for the use of the in-house, off-line computer system from those required for the use of the time-sharing system. The difference between the manhours required for the in-house off-line computer system and those required for the manual computation is also calculated for reference. If one plots the required manhours according to the three different systems, then it is possible to measure the marginality and value of each system.

The benefit is usually judged from two viewpoints. One is an absolute manhours' saving, and the other is a figure reflecting the difference between two systems. This judgment presupposes that, first of all, a certain value of manhours' saving is acceptable, and, second, that a certain degree of difference can make the system with the higher saving more advantageous. The bigger the difference, the more likely the system with the higher figure is to be selected.

This benefit aspect of the comparison is, however, not enough. Even if the benefit is great, a decision maker would be hesitatnt to select the system if the total cost of the system is correspondingly high. Thus, the cost side of the comparison is made next.

Development of the cost requires, first of all, comparison between the cost of the manual system and the in-house, off-line computer system. It can be easily recognized that even where the in-house, off-line system is to be utilized, personnel assistance is needed to execute the four jobs mentioned before. Therefore, the primary comparison is between the number of personnel required to handle the model development manually (with the use of desk calculators) and the number required for using the in-house off-line computer. Then human power requirements for the in-house off-line computer use are further compared to those of a time-sharing use.

More specifically, in the primary comparison, the factors relating to the manual system are:
1. Salaries for personnel.
2. Costs in regard to desk calculators.
And for the in-house off-line computer use, the relevant factors are:
1. Salaries for personnel.
2. Keypunching cost.
3. C.P.U. time cost.
4. Operation time cost (operator time cost).
5. System coordinator time cost.
6. Prorated program package cost.[23]
A crucial point to explore is the difference in the number of assistant person-

nel and the time required to obtain the whole output. If the number of assistant personnel for both systems is almost the same, and the difference in the total costs is substantial, then the choice would be the manual system, unless the time required to obtain the whole output is significantly different. On the other hand, if the difference in the number of assistant personnel is minimal and that in total costs is insignificant, the choice would be the in-house off-line system, that is, if the time saved by the off-line system is important.

In the second comparison, the factors to be considered for the on-line time-sharing system are:

1. Terminal equipment cost.
2. Telephone line installation on utilization charge.
3. Terminal connection time charge.
4. C.P.U. time cost.
5. Working storage cost.

Items 3 and 4 can be expressed in terms of dollars per hour and dollars per second. Hence, the estimates per month or per year can be computed to obtain the same basis for comparison.

The comparison between using the in-house batch processing system and installing a new time-sharing system weighs the dollars to be spent against the speed and efficiency of the modeling project. Suppose that the total costs of the off-line computer system and the proposed time-sharing system are $1,000 and $1,500, respectively. The core of the decision is whether or not faster completion and more precise analyses with the model are worth more than the difference between $1,000 and $1,500, that is, $500. Although there are many intangible factors—corporate traditions, informal power structures, and particular relationships with a certain company—to be considered after this basic comparison, a discussion can then be made as to whether to adopt the time-sharing system in place of the existing system or to continue using the present system. Furthermore, if a decision is made to install a time-sharing system, there remains the need to compare the various time-sharing systems available to the model builder and user. To make an approximate comparison there are a number of important factors to be considered.

The Relationship with Presently Available Systems

If the system of a firm is constructed from the hardware and software produced by a certain company, a new time-sharing system is likely to be the one from that same company, even if it is objectively compared to other systems. The extensive acquaintance of system management personnel and experienced programmers with a present system favors its expansion unless many disadvantages have been found to apply to it. Nevertheless, analysis of systems in depth (particularly with regard to their meeting objectives and performance) is necessary, even if the influence of a present system is substantial. One should be careful not to exaggerate the advantages and to ignore the disadvantages (particularly of a present system).

CONCLUSION

To evaluate the contribution of corporate models to the planning-organizing-control process, two considerations are basic: the possible contribution of control models to the planning-organizing-control process, and the possible continued use and improvement of present systems with those models. Control models can supply some important bases for policy decisions. These bases can be evaluated according to their use in budgetary planning, as well as according to more fundamental considerations such as the reliability of sets of figures predicted from them, and the useability, predictability, and suggestibility of the models can lead to the improvement and expansion of existing systems is illustrated by the application of FORPLANCON at INCO. The improvement of present systems is effected through the more cost-effective of two alternatives: application of the most cost-effective time-sharing system, or an in-house batch-processing system.

The selection of a new time-sharing system is a complex procedure. But as the user delineates his expectations of the time-sharing system, the many possibilities are resolved into one best alternative. To find the best system, both user and the model builder need to define important factors, collect necessary data, establish a certain model within the user's requirements, and evaluate the alternatives. time-sharing system is consistent with long-term system development planning and programming.

SUPPLEMENTARY READINGS

1. Fient, H. G. "Management of the Acquisition Process for Software Products," *Management Informatics*, Vol. 2, No. 3, 1973, 153-64.
2. Hammond, J. S. "Do's and Don'ts of Computer Models for Planning," *The Harvard Business Review*, March-April, 1974.
3. Jones, M. M., and McLean, E. R. "Management Problems in Large Scale Software Development Projects," *Sloan Management Review*, Vol. 11, No. 3, 1970, 1-16.
4. Kay, R. H. "The Management and Organization of Large Scale Software Development Projects," AFIPS Conference Proceedings (SJCC), 34, Montvale, New Jersey, AFIPS Press, 425-33.
5. Lucas, Henry C., Jr. *Toward Creative Systems Design*. New York and London: Columbia University Press, 1974.

REVIEW QUESTIONS AND PROBLEMS

1. What limitations must a prospective user or an executive be aware of before he requests a model builder to design and construct a model?

2. What considerations should the executive take into account when he finds himdself with a model unable to fulfill his requirements?

3. How can the existing corporate model help in the process of identifying the specific information requirements of the model user?

4. What functions are encompassed in the "management cycle" of your organization?

5. How do the business functions differ from headquarters to the various divisions of your organization?

6. How can a financial planning and control model be incorporated into your financial planning and control process on a periodic basis?

7. Does a corporate manager have some basis for evaluating material differnces between the figures presented by headquarters and those of division managers, both of which are based on the same corporate guidelines?

8. In what ways has progress toward the establishment of multiple goals been made in your company to date?

9. What are the methods of control in the attainment of multiple goals and how have they been executed?

10. How could the output of a computerized corporate financial model contribute to the guidance and control of your organization?

11. Explain four criteria or bases for evaluating a corporate model.

12. What considerations should be made when evaluating a predicted set of figures?

13. How is the allowable difference between the predicted figure and the corresponding indicator usually determined?

14. What are the six criteria given by Labovitz for determining statistical significance?

15. What additional criteria could be established for objectively determining statistical significance?

16. What questions must be asked in evaluating the data management process in general?

17. What are three criteria basic to a review of data collection and generation systems?

18. Within the framework of the planning-organizing-control process, in what way is required data classified?

19. How can all the data be exhibited in a manner that maintains the distinction between actual figures and predicted figures?

20. What is the meaning of the term "useability of the model?"

21. What is the key issue to discussing the predictability of information?

22. Is technological forecasting important in increasing the predictability of the model?

23. How do you define "suggestibility" in a computer-based corporate planning and control models?

24. What approaches do you suggest for the improvement of existing systems?

*25. What considerations should be specifically made in implementing existing systems?

NOTES

1. This chapter is based upon the author's paper in The Proceedings of the 13th Annual Technical Symposium sponsored by the Association for Computing Machinery, Institute for Computer Sciences and Technology, National Bureau of Standards, and U.S. Department of Commerce, June 20, 1974. For an executive guideline on the control of computers, see Lighton [21].

2. Much of the literature regarding corporate theory, analysis, and practice emphasizes the three functions—planning, organization, and control. Their implications for model construction are fundamentally similar, and they may therefore be examined collectively: hence the term "planning-organizing-control."

3. For budgeting and planning, see, for example, Schiff and Lewin [15] and Byrne, Charnes, Cooper, Davis, Gilford, ed. [16].

4. Error rate is defined as (Actual Figure in T minus Forecasted Figure in T-1)/(Actual Figure in T). Standard error of estimate is defined as the standard deviation used in setting confidence limits based on correlation, to explore how likely the regression curve and these relations are (as shown by the particular sample) to depart from the true values for the universe.

5. As of December 31, 1969, both forecasted figures by FORPLANCON and by division managers were compared. The error rate of FORPLANCON was 0.4% lower than that of division managers in forecasted premiums. The 0.4% amounted to $289,000.

6. For more details as to the probability figure (α), see Jensen [1], pp. 268-69.

7. Labovitz [2], pp. 220-22.

8. There exist various ways of classifying data into these three categories. Anthony [3], p. 19, classifies data related to strategic planning as planning data and data concerned with management and operational control as organizing and control data, respectively.

9. O'Brien [4] introduces varied exhibits in a decision center.

10. For the basic and applied reference for human factors, see McCormick [5] and Meister and Rabideau [6].

11. For example, see Desmonde [7].

12. Ibid., p. 3.

13. The earliest application of conversational graphic systems is usually considered the M.I.T. WHIRLWIND and the SAGE military command control system.

14. Green and Paislow [8], p. 35.

15. Ibid., p. 36.

16. The author is convinced that to increase the predictability of information requirements, technological forecasting is an inevitable area to explore.

17. Bright [9], p. 351. For example, Project HINDSIGHT analyzed the history of weapon systems development to discover significant factors in the development of defense technology [10] and Bright, op. cit., pp. 35-54.

18. Ibid., pp. 53-54.

19. See Jantsch [11], [12], and [13].

20. The questionnaire used by the writer in designing FORPLANCON contains the following:

Question 2: Please indicate some functional relationships you know empirically among various information mentioned above.

(Twenty-two different information items had been mentioned.) Responses to this questionnaire were of help in identifying key functional relationships decision makers or model users had used, and in examining the empirical accuracy of their descriptions of these functional relationships.

21. Shneeweiss [14], p. 475, contends that the decomposition in Figure 4.2 is due to a positive stationariness where $y(t)$ is not only stationary but also approximately Gaussian.

22. For basic concepts and application of computer timesharing for managers, see Haidinger and Richardson [22].

23. Although not specifically identified in this listing, sunk costs and existing capacity should not be ignored in the capital budgeting process.

CHAPTER V

Improvement and Extension of Existing Models

The objective of this chapter is to suggest improvements to existing models, and how these improvements can be implemented. Work on FORPLANCON and other models initially disclosed general areas for improvement, and subsequent research has permitted the identification and development of concepts and techniques which can facilitate the extension of existing models.

The specific improvements to be covered are techniques which can be used to improve the input and output aspects of corporate models. The first technique to be covered is feedforward planning and control. Application of this concept is suggested as a means to improve the predictability of a model. The second technique, the priority matrix, should permit a model builder to generate more effective outputs, including a more effective format. The third and final technique to be discussed is interval analysis. In many situations it is not possible to generate single figure estimates (for inputs and outputs). Interval analysis is a mathematical technique that contributes to a solution of such problems.

Obviously, there are many other techniques[1] that can help improve and extend existing models. Standard texts, reports, and papers on operation research, system analysis, system engineering, industrial engineering, information science, system science, computer science, decision science, administrative science, policy science, and related disciplines are worthy of being called attention in order to develop and apply a new technique to existing models.

Moreover, the improvement and extension of existing models can be made by:
1. Changing the type of a model from, e.g., the simulation model to an optimization model.
2. Adding more submodels and/or features to the existing models, e.g., to add a mixed integer programming submodel and post-optimal analysis routines.
3. Changing the timing of the model use, for example, to add to an interactive (graphic) model.
4. Using timesharing system(s) which enable(s) more users to use and evaluate the effectiveness of the model.
5. Strengthening the foundation of security management of the model system.[2]

FEEDFORWARD PLANNING AND CONTROL[3]

In the discussion (in Chapter IV) of benefits to be derived from corporate models, reference was made to the ability of a model to make predictions. At that time it was suggested that feedforward planning and control can contribute to improving the predictability of corporate models, and a discussion of the concept was undertaken. In the process of developing and operating FOR-PLANCON, the author was able to include application of certain aspects of the feedforward concept, and believes that it has significant application potential. For this reason, the concept and its application to model situations is elaborated herein.

Much has been written about organizational planning and control. The common plan-organize-control or, more simply, plan-do-see, description of management activities implies that the planning process precedes the control process. Control aspects are usually emphasized on the basis of observation of the control process in terms of feedback or adaptive control. In this context the objective of control is to reduce the difference between planned and actual performance. This involves negative feedback or a dynamic adaptive process wherein the a priori probabilities of attaining planned performance change as a result of a changing environment, and it also involves explicit decisions to readapt planning and control to these new probabilities.

When describing a control system or process, authors never fail to give attention to feedback control. Strangely, however, little attention has been given to a delineation and description of feedforward concepts or to the application of these concepts in management. This is even more surprising when it is realized that much of our knowledge about feedback concepts is the result of "borrowing" from engineering, and that it is in engineering, particularly in the area of process control, that feedforward concepts have been extensively applied.[4]

Definition of Feedforward Control

It is useful to define feedforward control on the basis of a contrast with feedback control—a term which has been defined in a variety of disciplines.

Forrester has defined feedback broadly by reference to an information-feedback system:

All information-feedback [control] system *exists* when the environment leads to a decision that results in action which affects the environment and thereby influences future decisions.[5]

This statement needs to be studied more as the raison d'etre of the feedback control concept than as a definition thereof. One of the important premises here is that the effects of an actual change in the environment determines future decisions, that is, a future decision is totally or substantially regulated by the actual change in the environment.

A committee of the American Institute of Electrical Engineers has supplied the following more specific definition:

... a feedback control system is a control system which tends to maintain a prescribed relationship of one system variable to another by comparing functions of these variables and using the *difference* as a means of control.[6]

In contrast to these two definitions which ignore feedforward control, Shinskey has comparative definitions of feedback and feedforward control systems. He regards feedback control as control which either augments an imbalance (positive) or works toward restoring balance (negative) between input and output through a controller. He defines feedforward control as control through which "The principal factors affecting the process are measured and, along with the set point,[7] are used in computing the correct output to meet current conditions. Whenever a disturbance occurs, corrective action starts immediately, to cancel the disturbance before it affects the controlled variable."[8] It is his interpretation that "Feedforward is theoretically capable of perfect control ... its performance only being limited by the accuracy of the measurements and computations."[9]

Shinskey illustrates a feedforward control system that includes a forward flow of information, and is regulated by a set point which permits anticipatory control, as in Figure 5.1.1. Koppel, on the other hand, describes feedforward control in terms of transfer functions, as in Figure 5.1.2, and says:

The feedforward scheme ... [illustrated in Figure 5.1.2] provides for direct measurement of the disturbance signal u(t) [an input reflecting a deviation from anticipated plan], and makes possible the use of this measurement to immediately provide a corrective manipulation to the process, $G_p(s)$, without waiting for an error signal.[10]

In the feedforward control system it is hoped to detect disturbances, and make steady-state corrective adjustments in the process so that the measurement of the controlled variable matches a reference (attainable) value.

The important differences between the feedforward and feedback concepts can be summarized as follows:

1. Feedforward control constitutes *ex ante*, that is, anticipatory control, whereas feedback control constitutes *ex post*, or follow-up control.
2. Feedforward control involves a forward flow of information, while feedback control involves both forward and backward flows of information.[11]
3. Feedforward control is realized before the control variables function, that is, before the difference between anticipated performance and actual performance occurs.
4. Feedforward control functions continuously in a given direction on the basis of the "command" of a set point, and is established at the time the user first feeds data into the model. In contrast, the frequency and relative importance of the flow of feedback control is a function of the change in the controlled variables.

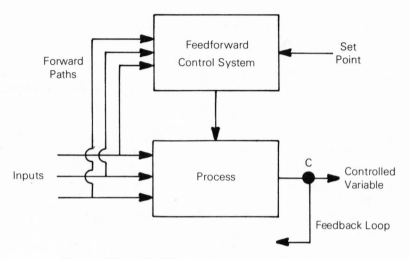

Figure 5.1.1. Feedforward control system.*

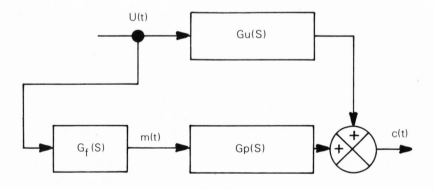

Figure 5.1.2. Typical diagram for
feedforward control.**

*Adapted from Shinsky, *op. cit.*
**Koppel, *op. cit.*, p. 23.

On the basis of these distinctions the author defines feedforward control as *anticipatory control in which preventive action is taken before the difference between planned and actual performance occurs*. This concept is very important for any organizational planning and control system, since a planning and control system, as shall be explained later, is future oriented in nature.

Feedforward Control vs. Other Control Concepts

In order to explain the more specific role of feedforward control in an organizational planning and control system, the author has chosen to differentiate it from other control concepts. However, because it is necessary to discuss control in relation to planning, the categorization to follow is one of planning and control concepts rather than simply one of control concepts. For purposes of the discussion, planning is defined as *determining objectives to be attained at a future target time on the basis of past performance in attaining identical or similar objectives*; and control as *the process of gearing for the attainment of objectives*.

1. *Zero-Order Planning and Control*[12] –see Figure 5.1.3. This occurs when planning at time t is exactly executed at time t + 1 as planned, i.e., the a priori performance vector equals the a posteriori performance vector. (In Figure 5.1.3, $P_t = P_{t+1}$). No control is necessary despite the time lapse. Predictable routine operations are examples.

2. *Feedback Planning and Control*—see Figure 5.1.4. This occurs when planning at time t is not executed at the time t + 1 as planned. Therefore, the difference between the *a priori* and *a posteriori* performance should be minimized through the control function. In this planning and control process, control commences after the deviation between two performances has been detected. Ordinary, corrective type inventory control is an example.

3. *Adaptive (Responsive) Planning and Control*—see Figure 5.1.5. This occurs when the deviation from planned performance is checked more readily (frequently) through control. If planning occurs at time t, and if a minor deviation or some sign of a deviation appear at t + Δt, the control function works at t + Δt so that the minor deviation may be nullified. This type of planning and control involves more cycles than feedback planning and control , that is, during a given time span, and involves a priori and a posteriori probabilistic considerations.[13] The living organism is an example.

4. *Feedforward Planning and control*—see Figure 5.1.6. This takes place when planning and control occur at time t before time t + 1 occurs. Hence the use of $\hat{P}_{t+1}$ rather than P_{t+1}. In this planning and control, therefore, planning itself is evaluated (planning evaluation) on an *a priori* basis as a result of anticipated environmental changes, that is, the control of time t + 1.

It is to be noted from the above discussion and illustrations that the important differences between a feedforward planning and control system and other systems relate to the timing of the control function and its relationship to the planning system.

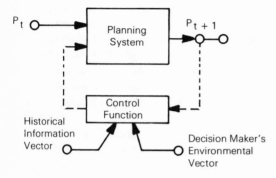

Figure 5.1.3. Zero-order planning
and control

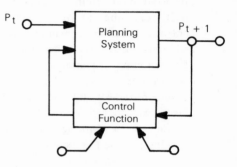

Figure 5.1.4. Feedback planning
and control

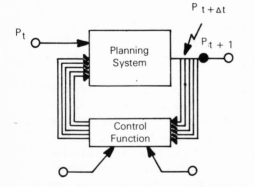

Figure 5.1.5. Adaptive (responsive)
planning and control

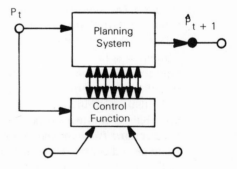

Figure 5.1.6. Feedforward planning
and control

Application of the Feedforward Concept

Successful application of the feedforward concept rests largely upon the design and construction of the planning system.

Discussion hereof can be undertaken by reference to a simplified (extrapolated) planning system in which a set of planning figures is determined simply on the basis of historical data. For example, if the number of employees (salesmen), annual salary per employee, and sales for divisions 1, 2, 3, . . . , n have changed year by year as shown in Tables 5.1.1, 5.1.2, and 5.1.3, then for this planning system, the estimates to be generated for the years 19X1, 19X2, and 19X3 are as given in the tables. 19X0 is assumed to be the base year.

Estimates for the above are generated from time series data.[14] For example, the computation for the number of employees for 19X1 would require determination and application of the most relevant and effective forecasting techniques. To illustrate, although the historical data often appear to be ostensibly neither linear nor nonlinear nor cyclical, detailed study of the data does disclose linear properties. Consequently, two regression approaches can be selected, linear regression and polynomial regression, and three selection criteria, standard error of estimate, F value, and residual properties. If the linear regression equation reveals a lower standard error of estimate, higher F value, and better residual properties than those of the polynomial regression equation, then we shall select the linear regression equation (but only after confirming that a sudden change of corporate policy is unlikely). Thus, we can determine the estimates $\hat{X}_{i \cdot t + 2}, \hat{X}_{i \cdot t + 3}$ on the basis of this equation.

In the above approach the estimates of experienced planners can be of undoubted help because of the likelihood of their ability to identify additional factors the importance of which cannot be recognized by an analyst. If enough data concerning these additional factors are available, it might be possible to identify a number of feasible functional relationships. However, it is ordinarily difficult to find enough data for identifying true relationships.

How would the control function operate in the above simplified planning system? As previously mentioned, one of the differentiating roles of control in a feedforward system is that of permitting an evaluation of planned figures prior to the occurrence of actual performance. An evaluation of the plan is especially necessary when certain control criteria need to be satisfied. Assume the existence of the following control criteria:

1. Total direct salaries should be minimized.
2. Total sales should increase by a stated percentage of the previous year.
3. The total number of employees is to be increased by a stated percentage of the previous year.

Given these control criteria, control commences with an evaluation of extrapolated figures of the plan against these criteria.

In this example, the required sales or productivity rate per employee for the years 19Y3-19X3 (arrived at by dividing total annual sales by total annual salesmen's salaries) is used as a standard coefficient to facilitate the development of

Table 5.1.1
NUMBER OF EMPLOYEES (SALESMEN)

Division	Actual						Estimate		
	19Y5	19Y6	19Y7	19Y8	19Y9	19X0	19X1	19X2	19X3
1	$x_{1\cdot t-5}$	$x_{1\cdot t-4}$	•	•	•	$\hat{x}_{1\cdot t}$	$\hat{x}_{1\cdot t+1}$	•	$\hat{x}_{1\cdot t+3}$
2	$x_{2\cdot t-5}$	$x_{2\cdot t-4}$	•	•	•	$\hat{x}_{2\cdot t}$	$\hat{x}_{2\cdot t+2}$	•	$\hat{x}_{2\cdot t+3}$
3	$x_{3\cdot t-5}$	$x_{3\cdot t-4}$	•	•	•	$\hat{x}_{3\cdot t}$	$\hat{x}_{3\cdot t+3}$	•	$\hat{x}_{3\cdot t+3}$
•	•	•	•	•	•	•	•	•	•
•	•	•	•	•	•	•	•	•	•
•	•	•	•	•	•	•	•	•	•
n	$x_{n\cdot t-5}$	$x_{n\cdot t-4}$	•	•	•	$\hat{x}_{n\cdot t}$	$\hat{x}_{n\cdot t+1}$	•	$\hat{x}_{n\cdot t+3}$

Table 5.1.2
ANNUAL SALARY PER EMPLOYEE

Division	Actual						Estimate		
	19Y5	19Y6	19Y7	19Y8	19Y9	19X0	19X1	19X2	19X3
1	$\bar{a}_{1\cdot t-5}$	$\bar{a}_{1\cdot t-4}$	•	•	•	$\overset{\Delta}{a}_{1\cdot t}$	$\overset{\Delta}{a}_{1\cdot t+1}$	•	$\overset{\Delta}{a}_{1\cdot t+3}$
2	$\bar{a}_{2\cdot t-5}$	$\bar{a}_{2\cdot t-4}$	•	•	•	$\overset{\Delta}{a}_{2\cdot t}$	$\overset{\Delta}{a}_{2\cdot t+1}$	•	$\overset{\Delta}{a}_{2\cdot t+3}$
3	$\bar{a}_{3\cdot t-5}$	$\bar{a}_{3\cdot t-4}$	•	•	•	$\overset{\Delta}{a}_{3\cdot t}$	$\overset{\Delta}{a}_{3\cdot t+1}$	•	$\overset{\Delta}{a}_{3\cdot t+3}$
•	•	•	•	•	•	•	•	•	•
•	•	•	•	•	•	•	•	•	•
•	•	•	•	•	•	•	•	•	•
n	$\bar{a}_{n\cdot t-5}$	$\bar{a}_{n\cdot t-4}$	•	•	•	$\overset{\Delta}{a}_{n\cdot t}$	$\overset{\Delta}{a}_{n\cdot t+1}$	•	$\overset{\Delta}{a}_{n\cdot t+3}$

Table 5.1.3
ANNUAL SALES

Division	Actual						Estimate		
	19Y5	19Y6	19Y7	19Y8	19Y9	19X0	19X1	19X2	19X3
1	$s_{1\cdot t-5}$	$s_{1\cdot t-4}$	•	•	•	•	$\hat{s}_{1\cdot t+1}$	•	$\hat{s}_{1\cdot t+3}$
2	$s_{2\cdot t-5}$	$s_{2\cdot t-4}$	•	•	•	•	$\hat{s}_{2\cdot t+1}$	•	$\hat{s}_{2\cdot t+3}$
3	$s_{3\cdot t-5}$	$s_{3\cdot t-4}$	•	•	•	•	$\hat{s}_{3\cdot t+1}$	•	$\hat{s}_{3\cdot t+3}$
•	•	•	•	•	•	•	•	•	•
•	•	•	•	•	•	•	•	•	•
•	•	•	•	•	•	•	•	•	•
n	$s_{n\cdot t-5}$	$s_{n\cdot t-4}$	•	•	•	•	$\hat{s}_{n\cdot t+1}$	•	$\hat{s}_{n\cdot t+3}$

the mathematical relationships. The operation of the control function can then be written, for example, in terms of an extremal method as shown in Appendix A.

By solving the linear programming formulation of the problem, we can determine the most desirable allocation of employees (number of) to each division. For example, suppose that the primary planning system has forecast (on the basis of a time series analysis) the number of salesmen for 19X1 as 35, 50, and 45 for divisions 1, 2, and 3, respectively, and that this represents an increase of five over the actual for each division during 19X0. Suppose further that feedforward linear programming has been applied to satisfy control policy and criteria, and that the revised estimate is 32, 37, and 40. Therefore, given a certain control policy and certain control criteria (without adding any new criteria or other factors), it is noted that the actual figures for 19X0 need to be increased by only two (as opposed to five) for divisions 1 and 2, while division 3 requires no increase at all. Further considerations might dictate a need to change even the 32, 37, and 40.[15]

This example implies that, when certain constraints exist, for example, company policy, there is no need to increase the number of salesmen of the less productive divisions. If one is able to rank the divisions on the basis of a productivity index or some other standard coefficient, then, for example, the number of salesmen of the highest ranking division should be increased first. And the increase should be up to the maximum number required for that division in the plan. The remaining divisions are attended to in the same way (in order of rank) until the number of salesmen allocated to divisions is adequate for purposes of accomplishing the sales goal. For a computerized model this recurring process can be summarized as follows:

Step 1: Find an average salary per employee in each division. (Use historical data and make an estimate for the future.)

Step 2: Find from the data base of the model a standard coefficient for each division. This can be done by using a subroutine, and a useful standard coefficient would be forecasted sales (dollars) per unit cost of an employee.

Step 3: Order the standard coefficients in a decreasing and/or increasing order.

Step 4: When additional employees are requested, assign them first to the upper limit of employees for the division that indicates the highest productivity coefficient.

Step 4-1: If the number of employees required by a division (to meet division goals) is equal to or greater than the total made available (by head office), allocate this available amount in full to the division and terminate allocation.

Step 4-2: If the number of employees required by a division is smaller than the total made available, allocate to this division to satisfy its requirements, and then proceed to allocate to other divisions in order of productivity until all available employees have been allocated.

Step 5: As time passes, find out if forecasted figures and productivity coefficients have been appropriately revised (periodically or whenever necessary).

Step 6: When a new allocation of new employees is necessary, start from Step 1, provided that Step 5 has been made on time.

Although, in this single example, only one year was considered, the allocation of employees can also be achieved under a multiyear situation. One of the crucial needs is an identification of the effect of the change over time (for any of a number of reasons) in the number of employees on the standard coefficients of divisions. The multiyear case is more likely to be affected by policy and decision variables (for example, a change in corporate strategy to diversify operations) which change the employee requirements of particular divisions, and this means that the standard coefficients are seldom stable. The effect of the change in the number of employees on internal (intraorganizational) factors should also be identified.

Once the optimum allocation of employees for each division has been determined (as above, the next step is to incorporate the result in, for example, a transfer allocation model, since the difference (assume a shortage for example) in the number of human resources should be taken care of by either hiring new employees or by transferring employees from division i to division j. The model is therefore a type of transportation model in which transportation costs (and the cost of new employees if applicable) should be minimized under certain policy constraints.

If, for example, the following objective function and policy constraints exist, as in Appendix B, then it is clear that the refinement of policy constraints determines the optimality regardless of the facts conveyed by new information. In some cases new information may change the objective function and policy constraints, but it must be recognized that this kind of feedback process is not solely an objective function and policy constraints formulation process. It should likewise be realized that, where the policy constraints of the transfer model affect the policy constraints of the model which made the initial allocation of employees, the latter allocation might have to be revised.

It might be useful at this stage to summarize the three distinct steps, in the total process above, of estimating for and allocating employees to divisions:

1. Initial estimates for the future are made on the basis of a time series analysis. The discussion included suggested use of one or two regression approaches (selected on the basis of three criteria). This step was undertaken within the scope of the planning system.

2. Feedforward control was applied in order to revise the initial estimates. The operation of the control function was described in terms of an extremal method.

3. A transfer allocation model was applied in order to minimize transportation costs. This step, like the second step, is part of the control function.

In the above example, linear programming is an integral part of the control process, that is, it is used to change figures in an original plan prior to actual performance. This means that an evaluation of the initial output (plan) is performed on the basis of feedforward control (as illustrated in Figure 5.1.7). The

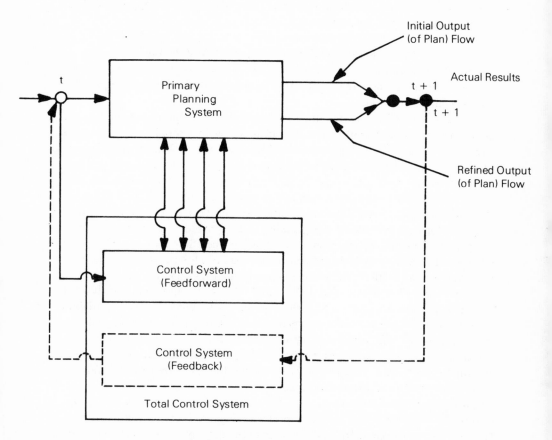

Figure 5.1.7. Application of feedforward control.

result is a refined output (plan).[16] In Figure 5.1.7, the dotted lines represent feedback flow and also illustrate the interaction between the feedback and the feedforward control systems. From Figure 5.1.7 it is clear that the control function can either include both feedback and feedforward control in one function block or consist of two separate function blocks.[17] Figure 5.1.7 also clearly shows the relationship between the initial and refined output flows.

Although in the above simplified example a priori type linear programming was used, the control function can be made to operate in such a way as to meet other system requirements,[18] such as:

1. Optimizing (maximizing or minimizing).
2. Ordering (ranking in ascending or descending order).

3. Changing of constraints (adding or deleting constraints).
4. Changing of variables (adding or deleting variables).
5. Changing reporting formats.
6. Selecting the appropriate approaches (hopefully the most appropriate) for meeting system requirements.

Evaluation of Feedforward's Application Potential

From the above discussion it is clear that in a feedforward system primary attention should be directed to the relationship between the planning system and the control function.

The suggestion of the above discussion is that the planning system can and should become more sophisticated. The planning system should grow in such a way as to increasingly incorporate control aspects. This implies an integration of part of the control function with the planning system. If this degree of sophistication is accomplished it might be useful to refer to a planning-and-control system rather than a planning system *and* a control system.

If the planning system includes a minor or substantial part of the control function (for example, where the planning system includes an optimizing function), there remains the question concerning the specific nature of the control function. The answer is still that control consists of an evaluation of the plan. For example, after the number of salesmen and total amount of salaries are projected for 19X1, 19X2, and 19X3 on the basis of a time series analysis, it becomes necessary to identify the other variables with which these two variables interact as well as their functional relationships. A revision of the original estimate of salesmen and salaries might then be called for. This evaluation process which dictates the need for a revision of the plan is then the nature of the control function. And the process is set in motion by a feedforward flow of information, before actual performance.

Control therefore functions through the addition or deletion of variables, constraints, or equations. Use of linear programming produces an optimum plan. However, by using parametric programming (changing of parameters) or by examining the effect of a certain constraint (by changing the constraint itself) the optimum figure can be changed. This change produces a marginal optimum, providing an overall continuity holds.

In cases where the planning system includes the whole control function the answer remains that control functions to control this aggregate planning and control system. The aggregate system has thus become more intelligent, and the control function should likewise become more intelligent in order to regulate the system toward more efficient decision making.

Therefore, generally stated, as the planning system becomes more intelligent it includes more of the control function. In this way the planning and control system is formalized simultaneously, and the control function becomes more intelligent.

It can probably be argued that the process of revising plans which are generated on a time series basis is common in practice. This is true, but feedforward control permits a finer delineation between planning and control, and a more appropriate relationship between planning and control. What has traditionally been regarded as the planning process is partially a planning and partially a control process. The control function is therefore larger than traditionally realized, and functions even as part of the planning process. Also, computers facilitate the process of evaluating plans frequently and on a continuous basis, and the definition and suggested application of feedforward control could contribute to the improvement of computerized corporate planning and control models. We have traditionally established plans and then awaited actual performance. The importance of feedforward control has been described, and model builders should now be aware of the need for and benefits of recursive evaluation of plans. This should result in the development of more feasible plans.

Generally speaking, feedforward control concepts will have application in strategic (long-range) planning, whereas feedback control concepts will continue to find application in tactical or operational planning and control. It should be recognized, however, that feedforward has applicability in even operational control situations—especially in cases where a controlled variable maintains a steady-state value. For example, since rent, depreciation, and certain salaries do not change at all (or change very slightly) from period to period, it is usually not difficult to predict the values of these variables precisely (or at least within an allowable range) for the immediate future. This information can therefore be supplied and used on the basis of feedforward control.

It also appears reasonable to the author to conclude that feedforward control concepts and techniques can be applied to situations which involve the establishment of a goal (plan) within a relatively large allowable range. For example, in connection with GNP there are two application possibilities. Assume that the United States sets its goal for 19X1 at one trillion dollars. Feedforward control can then function in order to make an evaluation as to the feasibility of one trillion dollars as a goal, and how much should be accomplished during what periods of time, and to reduce the range of the goal and provide information which will enable the establishment of a more specific figure if it is desired. This will occur during 19X0, and will be made possible by much analysis of data during the year. Feedback control will function during each of the periods, but only in response to actual performance.

An evaluation of feedforward planning and control is not complete without comment on its limitations:

1. The feedforward process is an evaluation process, and is concerned with the estimates of the uncertain future. This problem of uncertainty is likely to limit application of the concept.
2. It has only been recently that aspects of systems science, especially system control theory, have found application in business administration and/or accounting. It will take time for practitioners to accept the suggestion that feedforward control has application potential.

3. Study of the future (futuristics) is not well developed neither are the tools that have potential for overcoming the problem of uncertainty.

THE PRIORITY MATRIX

In Chapter III, the users' priorities as to information outputs were identified as one of the important development activities in constructing a corporate model. This particular activity has not been covered specifically in the literature to date, despite the fact that an appropriate approach to the problem is of paramount importance. The need for efficiency dictates that users' priorities be given attention. Work on FORPLANCON enabled the author to develop a technique, the priority matrix, to solve this problem.

A priority matrix is a matrix which indicates the order of priority in which various relevant data are required. It is, therefore, a representation of the model user's decision mechanism, including his preferences and all possible relationships among dependent and independent variables.

Table 5.2.1 shows that in a priority matrix each information element in the vertical columns is not necessarily the same as in the horizontal rows. Generally, the priority matrix is an m x n matrix. Diagonal elements (x_{ii}) do not occur in such a matrix.

Design and Construction of the Priority Matrix

In order to design and construct a priority matrix, the decision maker or model user must identify all his information requirements. The model builder, in turn, must analyse these requirements on the basis of a finite number of information elements. If it is impossible for the model builder to arrive at elemental data, he may have to settle for complex products which, with further examination, conceivably could be further analyzed into simple products.[19] Independent variables (changing factors) and dependent variables (affected factors) are thus identified and incorporated appropriately into both rows and columns. If the relative priorities for securing data on changing factors is identified, the required information element with highest priority is indicated in the uppermost column. The required information elements with highest priority are accordingly the first to be diagnosed.

Once changing factors and affected factors have been set down, the next step is to assign the numerical order of priority of each affected factor—1 through 8 in rows 1, 2, and 4 of Table 5.2.1. This step identifies the following:

1. The function relationships to be established;
2. The order in which the functional relationships are to be established;
3. The scope within which functional relationships are to be considered, that is, the rank of priority of relationships within which the determination of relationships is meaningful. Table 5.2.1 requires establishment of relationships only within the eighth degree of priority, since eight is the highest number.

Accordingly, if functional relationships between two information elements at a time can be established with no more than the allowable degree of error by a linear regression analysis, then a calculation chain[20] can be constructed, provided that a table of intercepts and regression coefficients (Table 5.2.2)[21] is already given.

Obviously, as in Table 5.2.1, the reliability of the results is a function of the stability of the changing factors. The applicability of a calculated functional relationship must always be verified.

Ranking informational items and recording the priority numbers of functional relationships to be diagnosed is the final step in constructing the priority matrix.

Of course, the construction of each particular decision matrix may require variations of this basic process. For example, it may not be feasible to incorporate all priorities into one table. Furthermore, priorities and the scope of the matrix may change as time elapses. One solution is to construct two or three alternative matrices in situations where the necessary adaptations of the original table are limited. Another approach is to construct the priority matrix listing only one information element horizontally, and indicating the several possible alternative priorities of its functional relationships with the elements in the vertical columns; thereby most alternatives can be included. Moreover, if the future status of priorities is uncertain but the matrix is required to retain as much validity as possible, the builder may construct a probabilistically founded matrix (Table 5.2.3) instead of constructing the deterministically based priority matrix. This matrix is like Table 5.2.1, but the probability of priority for each item is attached.

Value of a Priority Matrix

The advantages of the priority matrix are as follows:

1. The priority matrix transforms the model user's decision mechanism to a quantifiable, machine-workable format.
2. In the priority matrix, information requirements are stated in their most basic form; therefore, misunderstanding between model users and builders is eliminated.
3. The priority matrix can be adapted by increasing alternatives or by using a stochastic foundation (especially in situations where changes in the number and scope are likely).

The INCO Matrix

The priority matrix developed for INCO is an adaptation of the basic format, and is illustrated by Table 5.2.4. This matrix is not square, that is, m x n.

If the figure for vehicle premiums written is changed, the matrix is so constructed that vehicle policies in force, auto premiums written, number of employees, total direct salaries, payroll taxes, fringe benefits, total payroll costs, and total cost are changed according to a preference order based upon the user's perception of priorities. Other figures might be affected and changed accordingly; however, they do not concern the user. If an analyst finds another im-

Table 5.2.1
ILLUSTRATION OF A PRIORITY MATRIX

Independent Variable (Changing Factor) \ Dependent Variable (Affected Factors)	Column Information Element I	Column Information Element II	Column Information Element III	Column Information Element IV	Column Information Element V	Column Information Element VI	Column Information Element VII	Column Information Element VIII	Column Information Element IX	Column Information Element X	Column Information Element XI	Column Information Element XII	Column Information Element XIII	Column Information Element	Column Information Element	Column Information Element	Column Information Element XXXV
Row Information Element I	2	2		1		4	3					8	7	6	5		
Row Information Element II	2			1		4	3					8	7	6	5		
Row Information Element III						2	1					6	5	4	3		
Row Information Element IV	1	2				4	3					8	7	6	5		
Row Information Element V	1	2															

Dependent Variable (Affected Factors)

Independent Variable (Changing Factor)

	Column Information Element I	Column Information Element II	Column Information Element III	Column Information Element IV	Column Information Element V	Column Information Element VI	Column Information Element VII	Column Information Element VIII	Column Information Element IX	Column Information Element X	Column Information Element XI	Column Information Element XII	Column Information Element XIII	Column Information Element	Column Information Element	Column Information Element	Column Information Element XXXV
Row Information Element VI												2	1				
Row Information Element VII												4	3	2	1		
Row Information Element VIII												2	1				
Row Information Element IX												2	1				
Row Information Element												1					
Row Information Element												1					
Row Information Element XXX																	

C1	C2	C3	C4	C5	C6	C7	C8	C9	C10	C11
	34296 2.523	26178 4.854	7 .002	30759 7.287	5951 .172	1146 .419	-3134 .867	15461 -.401	22225 10.216	
-13426 .394		39588 1.921	-20 .001	67300 2.873	8404 070	-4079 .159	-14499 .337	20843 - 158	17846 4.052	9187 4.033
-5305 .205	20701 .520		-5 .0004	-9507 1.513		-855 .083	-33802 2.103	17603 082	-33802 2.103	-8721 2.100
				18813 33.195	6457 -85.836	1683 * 148.810	-3952 374.125	15778 -170.759	3562 581.402	27887 97.05
									-9356 1,292	13792 1.307
			16 .003	67086 11.522		1090 1.394	13464 -.633	73632 15.790	98450 15.782	
			10 004	44670 1.531		-1529 .185	14694 -.084	42486 2.108	67399 2.105	-1893 .132
									122308 38.933	
-101711 15.619										
32680 -3.230										
				-28028 451.138			18653 -24.674	-9862 52.842	-59055 25.594	-3381 24.158
										17194 -4.451
										73546 6.430
										28909 10.55
									128160 3.357	15311 3.338
									10.091 * 4.160	12572 4.082
										16954 47.21
				-4740 .296						
				984 .173						
				-2906 .336						
				6662 .195						

Table 5.2.2. Intercept

-3362				
.070				
-1952				
.051				

2693
28.885

1572*   -6654   5082*
.093*   1.026   .067*

14448   2606*
7.571   .220

-714
.039

Div. 19 Eastern
a. Intercept (Upper Hand of Each Box)
b. Regression Coefficient (Lower Hand of Each Box)

where $y = a_0 + a_1 x$

No Star: Credible
One Star: (*) Less Credible
Two Stars: (**) Incredible

regression coefficients.

Table 5.2.3.

ILLUSTRATION OF A PRIORITY MATRIX II

Independent Variable (Changing Factor)	Dependent Variable (Affected Factors) / Probability for Alternatives	Element I Column Information	Element II Column Information	Element III Column Information	Element IV Column Information	Element V Column Information	Element VI Column Information	Element VII Column Information	Element VIII Column Information	Element IX Column Information	Element X Column Information	Element XI Column Information	Element XII Column Information	Element XIII Column Information	Element Column Information	Element Column Information	Element Column Information	Element XXXV Column Information
Row Information Element I	0.43		1	2	3	4	5	6	7	8	9	10	11					35
Row Information Element II	0.25			2	1		3	4	5	6	7	8	9	10				
Row Information Element III	0.12		3	4	2	1			4		5		6	7				32
Row Information Element IV	0.06		5				2	1	6	6		7		8				12
Row Information Element V	0.05		2	3	4		5	6		1	7		8					

Independent Variable (Changing Factor) / Dependent Variable (Affected Factors) / Probability for Alternatives	Column Information Element I	Column Information Element II	Column Information Element III	Column Information Element IV	Column Information Element V	Column Information Element VI	Column Information Element VII	Column Information Element VIII	Column Information Element IX	Column Information Element X	Column Information Element XI	Column Information Element XII	Column Information Element XIII	Column Information Element	Column Information Element	Column Information Element	Column Information Element XXXV
Row Information Element VI — 0.03			1		2		3		4		5		6				10
Row Information Element VII — 0.02	3	2	1		4			5		6		7					
Row Information Element VIII — 0.02	4	3		2		5			6		1		7				8
Row Information Element IX																	
Row Information Element																	
Row Information Element XXX — 0.01			7			6		5	4	3	2		1				

portant functional relationship, he can augment the priority matrix. The more persons involved in the development of this table, the greater is the consensus as to priorities.

Once this table has been developed, the most significant functional relationship for each combination must be found by comparing each item with the items in the other column. For example, the most important relationship of auto premiums written with eight corresponding items is calculated. Assuming that predicted figures as well as present and past figures for each of them are available, it is possible to establish, one at a time, regression equations[22] (see Table 5.2.5 for explanation of symbols).

$$PW(VE)_{DI \cdot T+J} = K_{DI \cdot T+J}^{PW(VE)/PW(AU)} + R_{DI \cdot T+J}^{PW(VE)/PW(AU)} * PW(AU)_{DI \cdot T+J}$$

$$PF(VE)_{DI \cdot T+J} = K_{DI \cdot T+J}^{PF(VE)/PW(AU)} + R_{DI \cdot T+J}^{PF(VE)/PW(AU)} * PW(AU)_{DI \cdot T+J}$$

$$NE_{DI \cdot T+J} = K_{DI \cdot T+J}^{NE/PW(AU)} + R_{DI \cdot T+J}^{NE/PW(AU)} * PW(AU)_{DI \cdot T+J}$$

$$DS_{DI \cdot T+J} = K_{DI \cdot T+J}^{DS/PW(AU)} + R_{DI \cdot T+J}^{DS/PW(AU)} * PW(AU)_{DI \cdot T+J}$$

$$PT_{DI \cdot T+J} = K_{DI \cdot T+J}^{PT/PW(AU)} + R_{DI \cdot T+J}^{PT/PW(AU)} * PW(AU)_{DI \cdot T+J}$$

$$FB_{DI \cdot T+J} = K_{DI \cdot T+J}^{FB/PW(AU)} + R_{DI \cdot T+J}^{FB/PW(AU)} * PW(AU)_{DI \cdot T+J}$$

$$PC_{DI \cdot T+J} = K_{DI \cdot T+J}^{PC/PW(AU)} + R_{DI \cdot T+J}^{PC/PW(AU)} * PW(AU)_{DI \cdot T+J}$$

$$TC_{DI \cdot T+J} = K_{DI \cdot T+J}^{TC/PW(AU)} + R_{DI \cdot T+J}^{TC/TW(AU)} * PW(AU)_{DI \cdot T+J}$$

If multichange is taken into consideration,

$$PW(AU)_{DI \cdot T+J} = K_{DI \cdot T+J}^{PW(AU)/PW(VE) \cdot PF(VE) \cdot AP} + R_{DI \cdot T+J}^{PW(AU)/PW(VE)}$$

$$* PW(VE)_{DI \cdot T+J}$$

$$+ R_{DI \cdot T+J}^{PW(AU)/PF(VE)} * PF(VE)_{DI \cdot T+J}$$

$$+ R_{DI \cdot T+J}^{PW(AU)/AP} * AP_{DI \cdot T+J}$$

If a polynomial regression equation is established,

$$PW(AU)_{DI \cdot T+J} = K_{DI \cdot T+J}^{PW(VE)/PW(AU)} + R_{DI \cdot T+J}^{PW(VE)/PW(AU)} \left[PW(AU)_{PI \cdot T+J}\right]$$

$$+ Q_{DI \cdot T+J}^{PW(VE)/PW(AU)} \left[PW(AU)_{DI \cdot T+J}\right]^2$$

$$+ T_{DI \cdot T+J}^{PW(VE)/PW(AU)} \left[PW(AU)_{DI \cdot T+J}\right]^3$$

If an exponential smoothing approach[23] is taken, the coefficients in the multiple smoothing can be calculated as a linear combination of the smoothed statistics,[24] as is shown in Appendix C.

Moreover, if Gavor's self-teaching approach is taken,[25] comparing the mean-square error in the ith teaching step with the minimum error, it is possible to judge the quality of the representation of $PW(AU)_{DI \cdot T+J}$ for the chosen value of coefficients.

The extrapolation formula to determine the optimal value of the coefficient at R_i is given as follows:

$$R_i{}^* = \Phi \cdot \frac{\Delta'(R_i'''^2 - R_i''^2) + \Delta''(R_i'^2 - R''^2) + \Delta'''(R_i''^2 - R_i'^2)}{\Delta'(R_i''' - R_i'') + \Delta''(R_i' - R_i'') + \Delta'''(R_i'' - R_i')}$$

where Δ', Δ'', and Δ''' are three errors for three values of one of the coefficients R_i', R_i'', R_i''' and Φ is a coefficient derived from the condition of minimum of the mean-square error.

Hence, for Row i there is a certain ordered set. An attempt is made to find the major functional relationship of estimated information $\hat{i}$ (dependent variable) to estimated information $\hat{j}_k$ (independent variable) such that information i may be best described by j_k through some operator, such as a regression coefficient, smoothing constant, or weighting factor.

Although no one optimum criterion exists, if the standard error of estimate is chosen as a criterion for determining the most important functional relationship, then an operator such as regression coefficient is selected to satisfy the standard minimum error of estimate among various time-series data. When time-series data cannot be obtained, however, these functional approaches are unreliable. If time permits other approaches must be used.[26]

Table 5.2.4.

ILLUSTRATION OF INCO'S PRIORITY MATRIX

Independent Variable (Changing Independent) / Dependent Variable (Affected Factors)	Premiums Written –Vehicle	Premiums Written –Auto	Premiums Written –PLOTA	Vehicle Policies in Force	Average Premium per Policy	Total Direct Salaries	Number of Employees	Overtime Expenses	Temporary Help Expenses	Travel Expense	Telephone & Tele-graph Expense	Total Cost	Total Payroll Cost	Fringe Benefits Cost	Payroll Taxes	Rent & Equipment Cost	Employee Schools & Meetings Cost
Premiums Written –Vehicle		2		1		4	3					8	7	6	5		
Premiums Written –Auto	1			2		4	3					8	7	6	5		
Premiums Written –Other						2	1					6	5	4	3		
Vehicle Policies in Force	1	2				4	3					8	7	6	5		
Average Premium per Policy	1	2															
Total Direct Salaries												2	1				

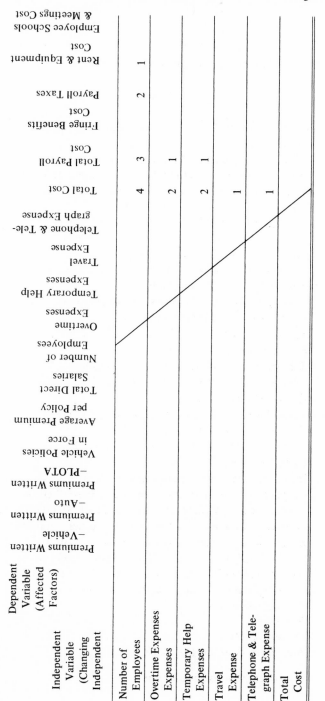

Independent Variable (Changing Independent) \ Dependent Variable (Affected Factors)	Premiums Written –Vehicle	Premiums Written –Auto	Premiums Written –PLOTA	Vehicle Policies in Force	Average Premium per Policy	Total Direct Salaries	Number of Employees	Overtime Expenses	Temporary Help Expenses	Travel Expense	Telephone & Telegraph Expense	Total Cost	Total Payroll Cost	Fringe Benefits Cost	Payroll Taxes	Rent & Equipment Cost	Employee Schools & Meetings Cost
Number of Employees												4	3		2	1	
Overtime Expenses												2	1				
Temporary Help Expenses												2	1				
Travel Expense												1					
Telephone & Telegraph Expense												1					
Total Cost																	

Table 5.2.5
THE MEANING OF EACH SYMBOL AND NOTATION

Symbol	Meaning
PW(VE) $_{DI \cdot T+J}$	Premiums Written for VEHICLE in Division I at T (standard year) + J
PW(PL) $_{DI \cdot T+J}$	Premiums Written for Others in Division I at T + J
PF(VE) $_{DI \cdot T+J}$	Policies in Force for VEHICLES in Division I at T + J
PE(AU) $_{DI \cdot T+J}$	Policies in Force Per Employee for Auto in Division I at T + J
$AP_{DI \cdot T+J}$	Average Premium Per Policy in Division I at T + J
$WI_{DI \cdot T+J}$	Number of employees in Division I at T + J
$DS_{DI \cdot T+J}$	Direct Salaries in Division I at T + J
PP(AU) $_{DI \cdot T+J}$	Premiums per Policy for Auto in Division I at T + J
$PT_{DI \cdot T+J}$	Payroll Taxes in Division I at T + J
$AS_{DI \cdot T+J}$	Average Salaries per Employee in Division I at T + J
$FB_{DI \cdot T+J}$	Fringe Benefits in Division I at T + J
$TR_{DI \cdot T+J}$	Transportation Costs in Division I at T + J
$PC_{DI \cdot T+J}$	Payroll Costs in Division I at T + J
$TT_{DI \cdot T+J}$	Telephone and Telegraph Costs in Division I at T + J
$TC_{DI \cdot T+J}$	Total Costs in Division I at T + J
$RE_{DI \cdot T+J}$	Rent in Division I at T + J
$SM_{DI \cdot T+J}$	Schools and Meetings Costs in Division I at T + J
$OT_{DI \cdot T+J}$	Overtime Costs in Division I at T + J
$TH_{DI \cdot T+J}$	Temporary Help Costs in Division I at T + J
$OC_{DI \cdot T+J}$	Other Costs in Division I at T + J
$K^{PW(VE)/PW(AU)}_{DI \cdot T+J}$	Intercept between premiums written (VEHICLE) (Dependent Variable) and premiums written (AUTO) (Independent Variable) in Division I at T(Standard Year) + J (the same rule is applied to other notations)
$R^{PW(VE)/PW(AU)}_{DI \cdot T+J}$	Regression coefficient between premiums written (VEHICLE) (Dependent Variable) and premiums written (AUTO) (Independent Variable) in Division I at T (Standard Year) + J (the same rule is applied to other notations)
+	Addition
*	Multiplication
a, β	Smoothing constant ($a = 1 - \beta$)
$S_t^{[\eta]}(z)$	Nth-order smoothing function

INTERVAL ANALYSIS

During the process of developing and operating FORPLANCON and other models, the author was often confronted with situations which prevented the generation of single figure estimates for inputs and outputs. It was found that users were satisfied with statements that a particular output was located within a range having an upper and a lower limit. In other words, users preferred outputs in such form rather than no output at all.

On the basis of this experience, the author believes that more attention needs to be given to this particular problem, and that the development of a technique that can be used to identify the appropriate upper and lower limits of a range should contribute substantially to improvement of the useability and predictability (see discussion in Chapter IV) of corporate models. During work on FOR-PLANCON, interval analysis was used to identify these limits. The basic approach, and suggestions for extension thereof, are described below.

In making estimates to be used as input for a corporate model, particularly a simulation model, the user often receives more practical results from applying a range, or interval, described by two figures, than from a point or a single figure. Uncertainties can often be most pragmatically described by estimated intervals—a range of possible figures—than by an estimated single point. Certain basic concepts of interval analysis are therefore relevant to the design and construction of corporate models.

The orderly quantitative analysis of ranges or intervals described by two figures in the fields of computer science and mathematics, have been undertaken by Sunaga,[27] Fischer,[28] Moore,[29,30] Boche,[31] Burford,[32] Ladner and Yohe,[33] and Griffith.[34] Basic concepts of interval analysis and properties of internal numbers are shown in Appendix D.

Practical Applications of Interval Analysis[35]

Interval analysis has broad application to the use of corporate models. Very uncertain estimates produce impractical outputs when stated as single figures. Rather, pessimistic, intermediate, and optimistic estimates, as in the PERT approach, may be fed in to produce the range of possibilities, thus facilitating contingency planning. In addition, probabilities may be attached to each input estimate, and thus to the output.

Whenever more than two estimates are indicated, interval analysis is a basic approach. The essential benefits of interval analysis are:
1. An estimate need not be considered a constant, but can be the width and magnitude of the interval. This enables us to see a number in the domain of a higher dimension.
2. The model user is aware of the difficulty experienced by a model builder in deriving the estimate. On the other hand, if the model user describes his requirements to the builder with interval figures rather than real number

constants, the builder can assume the feasibility of the width and magnitude of those numbers.

3. By using intervals which are known in advance to contain precise estimates, the significance of output numbers is more accurately represented. (This is an alternative to using inexact data and arithmetic.)

Moreover, using a digital computer to arrive at an exact solution is hardly possible, particularly when a rounding process is involved. But interval analysis produces boundaries of error between which the exact figure is known to lie. One example is described by Moore[36] in the form of a computation involving only a few arithmetic operations to debunk a frequently used method of estimating rounding error.[37]

Consider the recursion formula

$$X_{n+1} = X_n \text{ with } X_o = 1 - 10^{-21}$$

Computed using ten-place decimal arithmetic, the approximate values are

$$X_o = 1, X_1 = 1, ..., X_{75} = 1$$

Computed using twenty-place decimal arithmetic, the same approximate values are supposed to obtain, so that the two values for X_{75} in particular agree to all ten places in the first computation. However, the exact value is

$$X_{75} = (1-10^{-21})^{2^{75}} < (1-10^{-21})^{10^{22.5}}$$

or

$$X_{75} < [(1-10^{-21})^{10^{21}}]^{31.6} < e^{-31.6} < 10^{-10}$$

Interval analysis was applied to identify the scope of parametric change of each financial element by users of FORPLANCON. Since the scope of parametric change was given as a percentage, the financial elements were summarized by interval numbers, resulting in Table 5.3.1.

The benefits of this table are as follows:

(a) Model builders can reexamine the performance of the corporate model within the scope of parametric change.

(b) Model builders can more easily correct the performance of the model, when in fact the scope of parametric change goes beyond the original scope.

(c) Model users can more precisely assess changes in their parametric requirements.

The author's experience reveals that there is an observable preference among model users for representations by interval numbers as opposed to those by probabilities. The following two examples using interval estimates show the practical importance of taking into account the width and magnitude of an estimate.

Table 5.3.1
TABLE OF PARAMETRIC CHANGE

Division Information Element to be Changed	Southwestern Division		
	19X1 Estimates	Scope of Para- metric Change	Interval Number
Continuous Premiums Written — Auto	8,400	∓ 25%	[6300, 10,500]
Continuous Premiums Written — Other	3,800	∓ 25%	[2850, 4750]
Average Premiums per Policy — Auto	80.25	∓ 20%	[64.20, 96.30]
Average Premiums per Policy — Other	70.30	∓ 20%	[56.24, 84.36]
Number of Employees	25	+ 15%	[25, 29]
Total Direct Salaries	105,600	∓ 25%	[79,200, 132,000]
Travel Expense	2,500	+ 300% - 50%	[1,250, 7,500]
Telephone & Tele- graph Expense	3,520	+ 300% - 50%	[1,760, 10,560]
Rent & Equipment Expense	10,250	∓ 50%	[5,125, 15,375]
Employee Schools & Meetings Expense	515	+ 300%	[515, 1545]
Waived Items	3576	∓ 25%	[2682, 4470]
Overtime Costs	7600	+ 500% - 75%	[1900, 45,000]
Temporary Help Costs	18,400	+ 500% - 75%	[4600, 92,000]
Other Costs	10,730	+ 750% - 75%	

BREAKEVEN ANALYSIS USING INTERVAL ESTIMATES

The first example using interval estimates concerns a very simple breakeven analysis. The data used in this analysis is listed in Table 5.3.2. A hypothetical firm, Abacus Electronics, manufactures and sells widgets. The firm wishes to analyze the breakeven point for the data obtained from careful analyses of market prices and historical records. The estimates have been prepared, using the most optimistic and pessimistic assumptions. The arithmetic sum of all variable cost estimates defines the interval number for total variable costs. The same is true for fixed costs. The addition of interval estimates is not really different from ordinary addition. The three variables necessary for breakeven analysis are sales price, variable costs, and fixed costs. Table 5.3.2 also gives the "most likely" estimate for sales, variable costs and fixed costs. The "most likely" estimate is assumed to be the midpoint of the interval estimates. The results of a traditional breakeven analysis, using the most likely estimates, will be computed so that a comparison can be made with a breakeven analysis of the interval estimates.

Figure 5.3.1 contains the graphic and mathematical techniques employed in traditional breakeven analysis, utilizing the most likely estimates of sales, variable costs, and fixed costs. The breakeven point expressed in units of production and sales is approximately 489 widgets. By the most likely estimates, this volume is the best point estimate of breakeven, given the sales price and cost behavior described in Table 5.3.2. This analysis is very simple and easily understood, but it does not utilize all of the information available. If all of the available information is to be used in the analysis, then use must be made of the interval data.

A breakeven analysis, or more properly a breakeven interval analysis, of interval estimates will result in two breakeven points. These points are the lower and upper bounds of the breakeven interval. The formulas used in breakeven interval analysis are identical to those used in Figure 5.3.2. However, interval numbers are substituted for the point estimates. The calculation of contribution per widget is as follows:

Contribution per widget = Sales price per widget - Variable costs per widget
$$= [\$5.00 : 6.00] - [\$3.00 : 3.50]$$
$$= [\$1.50 : 3.00]$$

The interval estimates are enclosed in brackets, and, as illustrated in Appendix D, are used in arithmetic operations in much the same way as ordinary point estimates. The above result indicates that under the best expectations possible the contribution per widget will be $3.00. Under the worst circumstances the contribution will be $1.50. Using the midpoints of the interval estimates, the contribution is $2.25 per widget, or the midpoint of the above interval for the contribution per widget.

To continue the breakeven analysis, the contribution interval estimates must be incorporated into the computation of the breakeven points as to number of widgets.

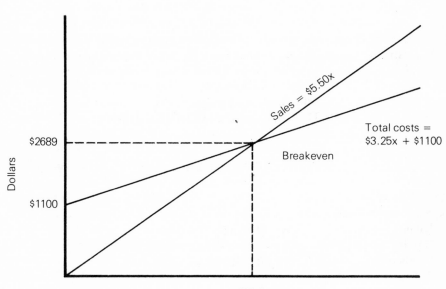

Figure 5.3.1. Traditional breakeven chart
using midpoints of interval data.

Breakeven in widgets = Fixed costs $\div$ Contribution per widget

$\quad$ = [\$1000 : 1200] $\div$ [\$1.50 : 3.00]

$\quad$ = [MIN $\dfrac{1000,}{1.50}\dfrac{1000,}{3.00}\dfrac{1200,}{1.50}\dfrac{1200}{3.00}$:

$\qquad$ MAX $\dfrac{1000,}{1.50}\dfrac{1000,}{3.00}\dfrac{1200,}{1.50}\dfrac{1200}{3.00}$]

$\quad$ = [333.3 : 800] widgets

The division of fixed costs by the contribution per widget, using the respective interval estimates, is slightly more complicated. Basically, the division of interval

Table 5.3.2
ABACUS ELECTRONICS, INC.
ESTIMATED DATA FOR 19X5 OPERATIONS[a]

	Interval Estimates[b]	Most Likely Estimate[c]
Sales price per widget		$[5.00 : 6.00]	$5.50
Variable costs per widget:			
Labor	$[1.00 : 1.15]		
Material	[1.40 : 1.60]		
Overhead	[.50 : .60]		
Selling	[.10 : .15]		
Total Variable Costs		[3.00 : 3.50]	3.25
Fixed costs:			
Manufacturing	[300 : 400]		
General	[500 : 550]		
Selling	[200 : 250]		
Total Fixed Costs		[1000 : 1200]	1100

[a]Sales price and variable costs per widget are assumed to be linearly related to the number of units produced and sold.

[b]The end numbers of the interval estimates enclosed by brackets represent the pessimistic and optimistic predictions but not necessarily in that order.

[c]The mid-points of the intervals are assumed to be the most likely estimates.

numbers involves selecting the minimum quotient as the lower bound of the breakeven interval estimate, and the maximum quotient as the upper bound. Note that the traditional breakeven analysis in Figure 5.3.2 yielded a point estimate that is within the endpoints of the breakeven interval, but it is not the midpoint of the interval.

To graphically illustrate the breakeven interval analysis results, the sales revenue and total cost curves for the interval estimates are plotted in Figure 5.3.1. Combining the optimistic interval estimates for variable and fixed costs results in a straight-line equation that forms the lower bound on the estimated total costs.

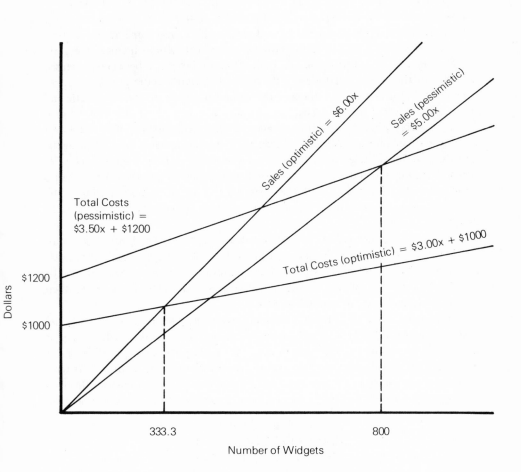

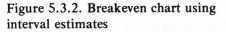

Figure 5.3.2. Breakeven chart using interval estimates

The pessimistic cost estimates form the upper bound. The sales price interval estimates are also used to form the boundaries for sales revenue. The optimistic sales curve consists of the higher interval estimate, and the pessimistic sales curve is the lower interval estimate.

The area bounded by the pessimistic and optimistic curves for sales and total costs contains the set of feasible breakeven points for the assumed revenue and cost behavior. The intersections of the curves define four possible breakeven points. The two extreme intersections, in terms of the number of widgets, represent the lower and upper limits of the breakeven interval analysis. The lower limit is at the intersection of the optimistic sales and cost predictions. The upper limit is at the intersection of the pessimistic estimates. The cost behavior and sales price projections are assumed to remain valid over this range of activity.

For the breakeven interval number, the width is 466.7, and the magnitude is 800. A smaller width would be more desirable. If management desires a lesser amount, they could reanalyze the cost behavior. This would increase the gathering costs of the information. A tradeoff must be made between increased accuracy of the interval analysis and the costs of gathering more precise data.

Figure 5.3.2 illustrates the impact on breakeven points of the pessimistic and optimistic sales revenue and cost projections. The impact of the interval estimates for sales price on profits can also be explored. Assume that the lower interval estimate for sales price will lead to a market demand for 2000 widgets, and that the higher sales price results in a demand for 1600 widgets. Each sales demand estimate could also be expressed as an interval number rather than a point estimate. For example, if the sales price is set at $5.00 per widget, the expected sales demand may be as high as 2100 widgets or as low as 1900 widgets.

The four combinations of sales demand expectations. Pessimistic and optimistic total-cost estimates are presented in Table 5.3.3. If the sales price is set at $6.00 per widget, and optimistic total costs prevail, then the maximum level of profit of $3800 will obtain. However, if the pessimistic total costs result, then profits could be lower by as much as $1000.

The data presented in Table 5.3.3 could have been generated from traditional cost-volume-profit analyses of all of the various combinations of sales and cost data. What would be the resulting profit if the sales price averaged $5.50, sales demand is 1800 widgets, and the pessimistic cost estimates are incurred? As with the breakeven interval analysis, the interval analysis of cost-volume-profit problems will set a lower and upper bound for each set of assumptions. Rather than

Table 5.3.3
ABACUS ELECTRONICS, INC.
PROFIT PLANS FOR 19X5

	Sales Price = $5 Sales Demand = 2000 widgets		Sales Price = $6 Sales Demand = 1600 widgets	
	Pessimistic	Optimistic	Pessimistic	Optimistic
Sales Revenue	$10,000	$10,000	$9,600	$9,600
Variable Costs	7,000	6,000	5,600	4,800
Profit				
Contribution	3,000	4,000	4,000	4,800
Fixed Costs	1,200	1,000	1,200	1,000
Operating				
Profit	$ 1,800	$ 2,000	$2,800	$3,800

complicating the results with probability estimates for the decision model's inputs, interval analysis simply results in an interval number, whose width and magnitude can be determined.

The width of the four profit estimates in Table 5.3.3 is $2000, and the magnitude is $3800. However, for the profit estimates resulting from a sales price of $6, the width is only $1000, and the magnitude remains $3800. Obviously, management would be more comfortable with the latter range of profits. The magnitude is higher and the width is lower. The interval analysis of cost-volume-profit data could also be illustrated graphically resembling the graph in Figure 5.3.2.

PRODUCT MIX DECISION MODELS

The previous section has illustrated the usefulness of interval estimates in breakeven analysis and its extensions. In this section, a two-product firm is assumed. What follows is a straightforward product mix problem in which total contribution profits must be maximized, given resource constraints. The optimization technique commonly employed to handle the product mix problem is mathematical programming. Three mathematical programming formulations of the product mix problem, using interval estimates, will be covered. The first illustration contains interval estimates for the objective function coefficients only. The second case adds interval estimates to the technological coefficients. Finally, the most complex of the illustrations contains interval estimates of the right-hand-side coefficients, in addition to interval estimates of the technological and objective function coefficients.

Example I: The first illustrative problem considers the case where the objective function coefficients (contribution profit per unit) are stated in terms of interval numbers. The general problem concerns a company that has undertaken to market two different products, and must determine how to maximize its profit contribution from them. Product A yields a contribution profit range of $2-5 per unit while Product B yields a range of $3-4 per unit. To produce Product A requires one hour of processing on work station one and two hours of processing on work station two. Product B requires two hours of processing on work station one, and one hour of processing on work station two. There are eight hours available on work station one, and ten hours on work station two.

Letting x_1 represent the number of units of Product A, and x_2 the number of units of Product B, the interval product mix problem is formulated as follows:

$$\text{Maximize:} \quad [2 : 5]x_1 + [3 : 4]x_2$$

Subject to:
$$x_1 + 2x_2 \leqslant 8$$
$$2x_1 + x_2 \leqslant 10$$
$$x_1, x_2 \geqslant 0$$

The optimum simplex solution to this mathematical programming problem is $x_1 = 4$ and $x_2 = 2$. Therefore, maximum profit contribution is $([2 : 5]4) + ([3 : 4]) = [8 : 20] + [6 : 8] = [14 : 28]$. The optimal solution in terms of the interval numbers provides the lower and upper limits of the maximum profit contribution, \$14 and \$28, respectively. If midpoints of the interval estimates are used as objective function coefficients, then optimal contribution profit will be \$21. The method of solving Example I can be easily adapted to other managerial cases. If interval estimates are desired for the parameters of the constraints, then the solution of the product mix problem is more complex.

Example II: Assume that the parameters of the technological coefficients of Example I are stated in interval numbers while the objective function and right-hand-side parameters are unchanged. To produce one unit of Product A requires a range of one to three hours of processing on work station one, and two to four hours on work station two. To produce one unit of Product B requires a range of two to four hours of processing on work station one and one to three hours of processing on work station two.

The interval problem formulation is as follows:

$$\text{Maximize:} \quad [2 : 5]x_1 + [3 : 4]x_2$$

Subject to:
$$[1 : 3]x_1 + [2 : 4]x_2 \leqslant 8$$
$$[2 : 4]x_1 + [1 : 3]x_2 \leqslant 10$$
$$x_1, x_2 \geqslant 0$$

The lower interval estimates for each of the technological coefficients are the same as the point estimates used in Example I. Therefore, two feasible results for profit contribution are \$14 and \$28. Other results could be obtained for each possible formulation of the product mix problem. A more efficient approach is to solve the interval problem directly, using available mathematical programming techniques.

In matrix algebra, the problem can be expressed as follows:

$$AX \leqslant B$$
$$A \leqslant X^{-1} B$$

Equivalently, in matrix form.

$$\begin{bmatrix} [1 : 3] & [2 : 4] \\ [2 : 4] & [1 : 3] \end{bmatrix} X \begin{bmatrix} x_1 \\ x_2 \end{bmatrix} \leqslant \begin{bmatrix} 8 \\ 10 \end{bmatrix}$$

Therefore,

$$\begin{bmatrix} x_1 \\ x_2 \end{bmatrix} \leqslant \begin{bmatrix} [1 : 3] & [2 : 4] \\ [2 : 4] & [1 : 3] \end{bmatrix}^{-1} X \begin{bmatrix} 8 \\ 10 \end{bmatrix}$$

Applying, for example, Cramer's rule for solving systems of linear equations, interval numbers are obtained for x_1 and x_2 as follows:[38]

$$x_1 = [\frac{16}{7} : 4]$$

$$x_2 = [\frac{2}{7} : 2]$$

The width of x_1 is equal to x_2. The width values are larger than those for the x_1 and x_2 in Example I. The maximum profit contribution is calculated as follows:

$$\text{Maximum Profit} = ([2 : 5] \, X[\frac{16}{7} : 4]) + ([3 : 4] X[\frac{2}{7} : 2])$$

$$= [5\frac{3}{7} : 28]$$

The optimal profit contribution given the interval technological coefficients is $28.00, while the lower bound is $5.43. The width and magnitude are $22.57 and $28.00, respectively. These values are larger than the width ($14), and same with the magnitude ($28) of the profit contribution interval number in Example I.

Example III: Assume further that the right-hand-side parameters in Example II are changed from 8 to [8 : 10], and 10 to [10 : 12]. These intervals indicate that there are eight to ten hours available on work station one and ten to twelve hours available on work station two. The other values of Example II remain unchanged. Therefore, the formulation contains interval numbers for the technological coefficients, the right-hand-sides, and in the objective function. The problem is obviously more complex and is formulated as follows:

$$\text{Maximize: } [2 : 5]x_1 + [3 : 4]x_2$$

Subject to:

$$[1 : 3]x_1 + [2 : 4]x_2 \leqslant [8 : 10]$$
$$[2 : 4]x_1 + [1 : 3]x_2 \leqslant [10 : 12]$$
$$x_1, x_2 \geqslant 0$$

Using the same computational approach used in solving for x_1 and x_2 in Example II, the following solutions are found:

$$x_1 = [\frac{16}{7} : \frac{14}{3}]$$

$$x_2 = [\frac{2}{7} : \frac{8}{3}]$$

Compared with the interval numbers for x_1 and x_2 obtained in Example II, the width and magnitude are larger by 2/3. The added variability of these interval number solutions is a result of the additional uncertainty concerning the right-hand-side parameters, which were increased. The upper interval estimates of available resources are two units larger than the point-estimates in Example II.

Substituting the obtained interval solutions for x_1 and x_2 in the objective function, the optimal contribution profit interval number is $[5\frac{3}{7} : 34]$. Thus, the optimal profits are higher than in Exhibit II, due to the increased resources available.

To simply validate the interval results of Example III, the problem can be reformulated, using the midpoints for each of the interval numbers:

$$\text{Maximize: } 3.5x_1 + 3.5x_2$$

Subject to:
$$2x_1 + 3x_2 \leqslant 9$$
$$3x_1 + 2x_2 \leqslant 11$$

solved as an ordinary simplex problem, the solution values obtained are $x_1 = 3$ and $x_2 = 1$. These point estimates are within the interval estimates for x_1 and x_2 in Example III. The optimal contribution profit is \$13. This point estimate is also within the range of the optimal interval solution obtained for Example III.

Potential of Interval Analysis

Predictions of the future have generally been represented stochastically or by estimated single figures. The increased use of interval analysis may obviate many of the problems arising from predictions based on only one of those methods.

The potential applications of interval analysis are many. All accounting or financial informaton which involves future uncertainty, but which can be identified by upper and lower bound figures, is subject to interval analysis. All sales, financial, production, research and development, personnel planning and control figures can be computed as interval numbers. Furthermore, interval numbers can be augmented with stochastic representations, if necessary.

Interval numbers are not only usable for input and output of most models. When a digital computer is used they provide a bounded result, which is more accurate than a single number constant rounded many times, no matter how many digits are carried.

Although some columns of a matrix may be reduced to zero when interval numbers are applied in Gaussian Elimination, this defect can be overcome by using interval numbers in Bisection, since there is no need to consider an additive or multiplicative inverse.

Although interval analysis hitherto has employed only two points, lower and upper limits, there is no need to so confine it. Some cases will involve more than two points. Therefore, development from single interval analysis into multiple interval analysis will be necessary, and this evaluation is comparable to the evolution from single dimensional analysis to multiple dimensional analysis.

CONCLUSION

A number of concepts and techniques for improving existing models and for implementing these improvements have emerged. In this chapter the main intent of the author has been to introduce some of the new concepts and techniques which have not been properly covered by other authors.

Feedforward planning and control concepts and techniques can undoubtedly help ascertain the importance and meaning of planning. They are suggested as means to improve on the predictability of a model.

The second technique, the priority matrix, can help a model builder to obtain more effective outputs, based on a user's decision criteria and preferences. The future potential of the priority matrix is immeasurable. It is suggested as a vehicle to improve on the useability and suggestibility of the model.

The third and final technique discussed is interval analysis. This technique can be useful in a variety of uncertain situations where it is not possible or desirable to generate single-figure estimates for inputs and outputs. It is suggested as a tool to improve on the reliability of the model.

APPENDIX A

EXTREMAL METHOD FOR OPERATION OF THE CONTROL FUNCTION

Objective function:

$$\sum_{ij}\sum \overset{\Delta}{a}_{i,t+j}\,\hat{x}_{i,t+j} = \sum_{ijor}\sum\sum\sum \overset{\Delta or}{a}_{i,t+j}\,.\overset{\wedge or}{x}_{i,t+j} \to Min$$

Subject to $\displaystyle\sum_{ij}\sum \hat{s}_{i,t+j} \geqslant \alpha \sum_{ij}\sum \hat{s}_{i,t+j-1}$ (policy constraint)

$$\sum_{ij}\sum \hat{x}_{i,t+j} \geqslant \sum_{j}\hat{x}{}^{*}_{t+j} \qquad \text{(policy constraint)}$$

$$\hat{s}_{i,t+j} \geqslant \overset{\Delta}{b}_{i,t+j}\,.\hat{x}_{i,t+j}$$

$$\hat{x}_{i\,t+j} \geqslant \sum_{or}\sum x^{or}_{i,t+j}$$

$$\overset{\Delta}{a}_{i,t+j}\cdot \overset{\Delta}{b}_{i,t+j},\,\hat{x}_{i,t+j} > 0$$

Conversely, for maximization purposes,

$$\sum_{ij}\sum \hat{s}_{i,t+j} = \sum_{ij}\sum \overset{\Delta}{b}_{i,t+j}\,\hat{x}_{i,t+j} \to Max$$

Subject to $\displaystyle\sum_{ij}\sum \overset{\Delta}{a}_{i,t+j}\,\hat{x}_{i,t+j} \leqslant \beta\sum_{ij}\sum \overset{\Delta}{a}_{i,t+j-1}\,\hat{x}_{i,t+j-1}$ (policy constraint)

$$\sum_{ij}\sum \hat{x}_{i,t+j} \leqslant \sum_{j}\hat{x}{}^{*}_{t+j}$$

$$\sum_{or}\sum \overset{\wedge or}{x}_{i,t+j} \leqslant \hat{x}_{i,t+j}$$

$$\sum_{ij}\sum \overset{\Delta}{a}_{i,t-j} \leqslant \sum_{j}\overset{\wedge *}{a}_{t+j}$$

$$\overset{\Delta}{a}_{i,t+j},\,\overset{\Delta}{b}_{i,t+j},\,\hat{x}_{i,t+j} > 0$$

where $\overset{\Delta}{a}_{i,t+j}$: Estimated Average Annual Salary for Division i at Year $t+j$

$\overset{\Delta or}{a}_{i,t+j}$: Estimated Average Annual Salary of an Employee with Rank r in Job Title o for Division i at Year $t+j$
(The use of suffixes is applicable to other symbols.)

$\hat{x}_{i,t+j}$: Estimated Number of Employees for Division i at Year $t+j$

$\hat{s}_{i,t+j}$: Estimated Total Sales for Division i at Year $t+j$

$\overset{\Delta}{b}_{i,t+j}$: Estimated Average Productivity per Employee for Division i at Year $t+j$

α, β : Policy Coefficients

$\hat{x}^*_{t+j}$: Estimate of Total Number of Employees at Year $t + j$ determined discretionarily by an organizational policy

$\hat{a}^*_{t+j}$: Estimate of Total Annual Salaries at Year $t + j$ derived discretionarily by an organizational policy

APPENDIX B

OBJECTIVE FUNCTIONS AND POLICY CONSTRAINT FOR ALLOCATION OF EMPLOYEES

Objective function:

$$P^{or}_{ij,t+k} \underset{ijkor}{\Sigma\Sigma\Sigma\Sigma} \left[\widehat{(TE)}^{or}_{ij,t+k} + \widehat{(ME)}^{or}_{ij,t+k} \right] + P^{r \to s}_{ij,t+1}$$

$$\underset{sijor}{\Sigma\Sigma\Sigma\Sigma\Sigma} \left[\widehat{(DS)}^{os}_{ij,t+1} - \widehat{(DS)}^{or}_{ij,t+1} \right] \longrightarrow \text{Min}$$

Subject to $\delta \underset{ijkor}{\Sigma\Sigma\Sigma\Sigma\Sigma} \left[\widehat{(TE)}^{or}_{ij,t+k} + \widehat{(ME)}^{or}_{ij,t+k} \right] + \eta \underset{ijors}{\Sigma\Sigma\Sigma\Sigma\Sigma}$

$$\left[\widehat{(DS)}^{os}_{ij,t+1} - \widehat{(DS)}^{or}_{ij,t+1} \right] \leqq \underset{ik}{\Sigma\Sigma} (TC)^*_{i,t+k} \text{ (policy constraint)}$$

$$\underset{ijk}{\Sigma\Sigma\Sigma} P^m_{ij,t+k} \cdot \widehat{M}_{t+k} \leq \underset{k}{\Sigma} \widehat{M}^*_{t+k} \text{ (policy constraint)}$$

$$P^{r \to s}_{ij,t+k} \cdot \underset{ijkor}{\Sigma\Sigma\Sigma\Sigma\Sigma} \left[(DS)^{os}_{ij,t+1} - (DS)^{or}_{ij,t} \right]$$

$$x \left[(DS)^{TOT}_t \right]^{-1}$$

$$\leqq P^{r \to s}_{ij,t+k} \cdot \underset{ijkor}{\Sigma\Sigma\Sigma\Sigma\Sigma} \left[\widehat{(DS)}^{os}_{ij,t} - (DS)^{or}_{ij,t-1} \right]$$

$$x \left[(DS)^{TOT}_{t-1} \right]^{-1}$$

$$\delta \cdot \widehat{M}_{t+k}, \widehat{(TE)}^{or}_{ij,t+k}, \widehat{(ME)}^{or}_{ij,t+k},$$

$$\eta \cdot \widehat{(DS)}^{os}_{ij,t+1}, \widehat{(DS)}^{or}_{ij,t+1}, \widehat{(TC)}_{i,t+k}$$

$$(DS)_{ij,t} \geqslant 0$$

$$0 \leqslant P^m_{ij,t+k} \leqslant 1$$

$$0 \leqslant P_{ij}^{r \rightarrow s} \leqslant 1$$

$$0 \leqslant P_{ij,t+k}^{or} \leqslant 1$$

where

$P_{ij,t+k}^{or}$: Probability of transferring from Division i to Division j for an employee with Rank r in Job Title O at Year $t + k$

$P_{ij,t+k}^{r \rightarrow s}$: Probability of Promotion from Rank r to Rank s (within the same job title) as a result of transfer from Division i to Division j at Year $t + k$

$\widehat{(TE)}$: Estimates of Transportation Expense

$\widehat{(ME)}$: Estimates of Moving Expense (in addition to Transportation Expense)

$\widehat{(DS)}$: Estimates of Direct Salaries

$\widehat{(TC)}^*$: Policy Estimates of Total Costs

$\alpha, \beta, \gamma, \delta, \eta,$: Policy Coefficients

$\widehat{M}_{t+k}$: Estimates of number of employees who transfer from Division i to Division j at Year $t + k$

APPENDIX C

SMOOTHING TECHNIQUES

In general,

$$PW(AU)_{DI \cdot T+J} = X_{T+J} = X_T^{(0)} + JX_T^{(1)} + 1/2J^2 X_T^{(2)}$$

$$+ \ldots + \frac{1}{n!} J^n X_T^{(n)}$$

$$= \sum_{k=0}^{n} J^k \frac{X_T^{(k)}}{K!}$$

Then

$$S_t^{[p]}(X) = \sum_{k=0}^{n} (-1)^k \frac{X_t^{(K)}}{K!} \cdot \frac{\alpha P}{(P-1)!} \sum_{j=0}^{\infty} j^K \beta^j \frac{(P-1+j)!}{j!}$$

More specifically,

1. Triple smoothing

$$PW(AU)_{DI \cdot T + J} = X_{T + J}$$

$$= a_0 + J_1 \cdot \hat{a}_1 (T) + 1/2J^2 \hat{a}_2 (T)$$

$$= [6\beta^2 + (6 - 5\alpha)\alpha J + \alpha^2 J^2] \frac{S_T(x)}{2\beta^2}$$

$$- [6\beta^2 + 2(5 - 4\alpha)\alpha J + 2\alpha^2 J^2] \frac{S_t^{[2]}(x)}{2\beta^2}$$

$$+ [2\beta^2 + (4 - 3\alpha)\alpha J + \alpha^2 J^2] \frac{S_t^{[3]}(x)}{2\beta^2}$$

2. Double smoothing

$$PW(AU)_{DI \cdot T + J} = X_{T + J}$$

$$= (2 + \frac{\alpha J}{B}) S_T(X) - (1 - \frac{\alpha J}{\beta})S_T^{[2]}(X)$$

where $S_o(X) = a_0(0) + \frac{\beta}{\alpha}a_1(0)$

$$S_0^{[2]}(X) = a_0(0) - \frac{2\beta}{\alpha} a_1(0)$$

3. Single smoothing

$$PW(AU)_{DI \cdot T + J} = a_0(T) + S_T(X)$$

$$S_t(X) = \alpha X(t) + \beta s_{t-1}(X)$$

APPENDIX D

Basic Concepts of Interval Analysis and Properties of Interval Numbers

Interval Numbers. Moore's work in interval analysis[39] provides good definitions of the basic properties of interval numbers. Moore defines an interval number, or simply, an interval, to be an ordered pair of real numbers, [a, b], with $a \leqslant b$. An interval number [a, b] is also a set of real numbers. The interval number [a, b] is the set of real numbers x such that $a \leqslant X \leqslant b$, that is,

$$[a, b] = [x | a \leq x \leq b] \tag{5.1}$$

He, therefore, defines the *width* of an interval [a, b] by

$$W([a, b]) = b - a \tag{5.2}$$

and the *magnitude* of an interval by

$$| [a, b] | = max(| a |, | b |) \tag{5.3}$$

A partial ordering of the elements of J^{40} is defined by

$$[a, b,] < [c, d] \text{ if and only if } b < c \tag{5.4}$$

If [a, b] = [c, d], then this means that a = c and b = d. Interval analysis thus implies operating throughout an algorithm with interval numbers rather than with real point figures or real number constants.

Exact-Interval Arithmetic. Arithmetic operations with intervals as defined by Moore[41] were developed from Dwyer's work on "range arithmetic."[42] Exact-interval arithmetic is fundamentally a variation of real arithmetic.[43]

If [a, b] and [c, d] are two interval numbers, and if * is one of the symbols, $+, -, x, \div$; then

except that $\dfrac{[a, b]}{[c, d]}$ is undefined if $0 \epsilon [c, d]$.

$$[a,b] * [c,d] = x*y \ x\epsilon [a,b], \ y\epsilon[c,d] = |x*y \ a\leq x \leq b, \ c \leq y \leq d] \tag{5.5}$$

From (5.5), an equivalent set of algebraic definitions, the sum, difference, product, or quotient of two intervals, is as follows:

$$[a, b] + [c, d] = [a+c, b+d]$$

$$[a, b] - [c, d] = [a-d, b-c]$$

$$[a, b] \ x \ [c, d] = [min \ (ac, ad, bc, bd),$$

$$max \ (ac, ad, bc, bd)]$$

$$[a, b] \div [c, d] = [a, b] \cdot [\tfrac{1}{d}, \tfrac{1}{c}]$$

$$\text{where } 0 \notin [c, d] \tag{5.6}$$

It follows from (5.6) that real number constants are a particular class of interval numbers, that is, degenerate interval numbers such that

$$[a, a] = (x | x\epsilon[a, a]) \equiv a \tag{5.7}$$

Interval arithmetic with degenerate intervals is ordinary arithmetic.

$$[a, a] + [b, b] = [a+b, a+b]$$
$$\equiv a + b$$
$$[a, a] - [b, b] = [a-b, a-b]$$
$$\equiv a - b \tag{5.8}$$

Associative and Commutative Properties. Since a, b, c, d are real numbers, interval addition and multiplication inherit the associative and commutative laws of all real numbers. Thus, for intervals I, J, K:

$$I + (J+K) = (I+J) + K \quad \text{(Associative)}$$
$$I \cdot (J \cdot K) = (I \cdot J) \cdot K \quad \text{(Associative)} \qquad (5.9)$$

$$I + J = J + I \quad \text{(Commutative)}$$
$$I \cdot J = J \cdot I \quad \text{(Commutative)} \qquad (5.10)$$

A proof of the associative and commutative properties of (5.9) and (5.10) can be found in the Appendix of Griffith's dissertation.

From (5.9) and (5.10) the corollaries follow:

A. The interval number [0,0] is the additive identity for interval arithmetic.[44]

B. The interval number [1,1] is the multiplicative identity for interval arithmetic.[45]

The distributive property of real numbers does not pertain to interval numbers exactly. The following computation exemplifies this condition:

$$[1, 2] \cdot ([1, 2] + [-2, -1]) = [1, 2] \cdot [-1, 1]$$
$$= [-2, 2]$$

whereas

$$([1, 2] \cdot [1, 2]) + ([1, 2] \cdot [-2, -1]) = [1, 4]$$
$$+ [-4, -1] = [-3, 3]$$

In relation to addition and multiplication, there exists the following subdistributive property for all intervals I, J, K,

$$I \cdot (J + K) \subset (I \cdot J) + (I \cdot K) \, {}^{[46]} \qquad (5.11)$$

And if J and K are intervals such that they contain real numbers of the same sign so that $J \cdot K > 0$, then

$$I \cdot (J + K) = (I \cdot J) + (I \cdot K)^{[47]}$$

On the other hand, if t is a real number, i.e., [t,t] , and I and J intervals, then,

$$t(I + J) = tI + tJ^{[48]}$$

Proofs of the above theorem and corollaries are contained in Burford.[49]

Monotonic Property. An operation "*" is said to be inclusion montonic if, given intervals $I \subset K, J \subset L$ we have

$$(I*J) \subset (K*L)^{[50]} \qquad (5.12)$$

That interval arithmetic is inclusion montonic is expressed as follows. Let, I, J, K, L be intervals such that $I \subset K$ and $J \subset L$. Then,

$$(I + J) \subset (K + L)$$
$$(I - J) \subset (K - L)$$
$$(I \cdot J) \subset (K \cdot L) \qquad (5.13)$$

and provided that

$$(I/J) \subset (K/L)^{51}$$

Proofs of the above definition and theorem are also presented in Burford.

Given the above properties of interval numbers, some of their practical applications can be demonstrated.

SUPPLEMENTARY READINGS

1. Couger, D. "Evolution of Business System Analysis Techniques," in Couger, D., and Knapp, R., ed. *System Analysis Techniques*. New York: John Wiley & Sons, Inc., 1974.
2. Koontz, H., and Bradspies, R. "Managing Through Feedforward Control," *Business Horizons*, June, 1972, 25-36.
3. Mitroff, I. "A Communication Model of Dialectical Inquiring Systems – A Stretegy for Strategic Planning," *Management Sciences*, Vol. 17, No. 10(June, 1971), B-634-B-648.
4. Sibley, E. H., and Merten, A. G. "Implementation of a Generalized Data Base Management System within an Organizaton," *Management Informatics*, Vol. 2, No. 1, 1973, 21-31.
5. Teichroew, D., and Sayani, H. "Automation of System Building," *Datamation*, Vol. 17, No. 16, 1971, 25-30.

REVIEW QUESTIONS AND PROBLEMS

1. What would you suggest to improve existing models. How can these improvements be implemented?

2. Why has little attention been given to the description and clarification of feedforward concepts or to the application of these concepts in management?

3. What are the essential differences between feedforward control systems and feedback control systems?

4. Give a theoretical definition of feedforward control.

5. State the differences among zero-order planning and control, feedback planning and control, adaptive (responsive) planning and control, and feedforward planning and control?

6. What are the main areas in which feedforward concepts can be applied?

7. Illustrate two or three applications of the feedforward concept, including conceivable control criteria?

8. In the case cited in this chapter, what are three distinct steps used for estimating and allocating employees to divisions?

9. Depict as clearly as possible the relationship between feedforward and feedback control system in a total control system?

10. How can the control function be made to operate in such a way as to meet system requirements?

11. Evaluate the application potential of feedforward planning and control systems? Classify feedforward systems on the basis of possible applications.

12. Do you agree or disagree with this statement? Is feedforward control nothing but planning? State your reasons.

13. Define a priority matrix.

14. How do you design and construct a priority matrix?

15. Define a calculation chain.

16. What are the differences between a priority matrix and a decision table?

17. What are the advantages and disadvantages of the priority matrix?

18. What technical approaches are directly related to the establishment of a priority matrix?

19. What is the main justification for making an interval analysis?

20. Describe and discuss basic concepts of interval analysis and properties of interval numbers.

21. What is exact-interval arithmetic? How does it differ from real arithmetic?

22. What is the most important characteristic of the distributive property of real numbers?

23. How could you apply interval analysis to your area of concern?

24. Do you think that interval analysis can be applied to contingency planning and control?

25. What are the essential merits and demerits of interval analysis?

26. How do you evaluate the flexibility of interval numbers and the results in Examples I, II and III of the text?

27. What do you believe to be the potential of interval analysis? What should be important considerations in applying and developing interval analysis?

*28. Summarize all the other concepts and techniques you think relevant for developing the corporate models.

NOTES

1. Several handbooks through which readers can get access to the information on techniques are Lazzaro(33), Maynard(34), Maynard(35), Hartman(36), Machol(46), Pearson(47), Claire(48), Korn and Korn(49), and Keppel(50).

2. Those topics will not be discussed further in this text. For security management, see, for example, Hoffman(42), Allen(43), and Bates(44).

3. This section is based upon Ishikawa and Smith [37] and [38].

4. See, for example, Shinskey [1], pp. 61-65; MacMullan and Shinskey [2], pp. 69-74; and Luyben and Gerster [3], pp. 374-81.

5. Forrester [4], p. 14. Emphasis added.

6. American Institute of Electrical Engineers Committee Report [5], p. 909. Emphasis added.

7. A set point is a type of "command" input which gives direction to the system. See Figure 5.1.1.

8. F. G. Shinskey [6], p. 205. A controlled variable is "that quantity or condition of the controlled system which is directly measured and controlled." See American Institute of Electrical Engineers Committee Report, op. cit.

9. Shinskey, ibid.

10. Koppel [7], p. 23. The overall relation between u(t) and c(t) (the input and the output signals, respectively, of the loop) is $c(s) = [G_u(s) + G_f G_p(s)] u(s)$.

11. This does not mean that feedback control encompasses feedforward control. The latter has a distinctive relationship to the planning system. This is elaborated in the next section.

12. Murphy has, for example, discussed a similar concept (he describes it as a Type O Process) with reference to economic systems. See, Murphy Jr. [8], p. 16.

13. Adaptive processes include properties such as the ability to enable the system to move off into any one of a number of different directions, and to adapt to the new environment, and decision-making functions operating under uncertainty (this requires stochastic representations on the part of a decision maker to the system and its environment), and sequential time processes. More specifically, an optimal adaptive control process exists if the following are given:

(a) An information pattern (such as a state vector).

(b) The a priori distribution function of the information pattern.

(c) An adaptation rule to be followed by the system.

The author's description of adaptive planning and control focuses on the frequency of control rather than the proporties mentioned above.

14. For applied time series analysis for forecasting, see, for example, Nelson [45].

15. It is anticipated that these figures become more stable or at least fall within a stable range, as the repetition of the feedforward linear programming continues with similar constraints and as the time horizon to be forecasted gets shorter.

16. Particular emphasis should be placed on the policy constraints which are likely to change. No "best" policy constraint exists in the real world, and the method for determining the policy constraints is, in some sense, the key for identifying how often, and to what extent, the feedforward process should operate.

17. Actually, most writers point out that feedforward control alone is inadequate for industrial processes because of its sensitivity to errors in the mathematical model. See, for example, McGuire [9]; Haskins and Sliepcevich [10], pp. 253-57 and pp. 241-48.

18. A linear programming model can be used as part of the control function. In addition, sensitivity or economic analysis of the LP model is a control technique and therefore part of the overall control function. On the subject of sensitivity analysis see, for example, Rappaport [11], pp. 441-56; Jensen [12], pp. 424-46, and Hartley [13], pp. 223-34.

19. When it is possible to find simple information, complex information may

be usable as semielemental information. Careful analysis must determine if such information can be used to attain the objectives of the corporate model.

20. A calculation chain means the recurring process of calculation that involves

(1) Identifying the initial formula to be calculated

(2) Executing calculation

(3) Obtaining a solution

(4) Identifying the next formula to be calculated

(5) Return to (2).

This continues until obtaining a solution from the final formula.

21. See page 169.

22. Needless to say, there are inherent weaknesses in regression analysis and therefore practicability of results must be examined carefully. For a useful discussion of application, use, and limitations of multiple regression analysis, see Benston [14], pp. 657-72.

23. Basic concepts of smoothing were developed by Brown [15]. As to more diversified approaches and monitoring discussion, see Gross and Ray [16] and Batty [17].

24. As to the workability of smoothing constant α, see Brown, op. cit., p. 121, for the exponential correlation function's case. The minimum mean square error

occurs when $\quad P = \dfrac{e^{-\lambda t} - (e^{-\lambda t}(1+e^{-\lambda}) - e^{-\lambda})^{\frac{1}{2}}}{e^{-\lambda} - e^{-\lambda t}}$

25. Gabor, Wilby, and Woodcock [18], pp. 422-38 and Ivakhnenko and Laya [19].

26. There are many other techniques in the area of forecasting and planning. See, for example, Jenkins and Watts [39], Wheelwright and Makridakis [40], and Box-Jenkins Models [41, pp. 8-10].

27. Sunaga [20].

28. Fisher [21].

29. Moore [22].

30. Moore [23].

31. Boche [24].

32. Burford [25].

33. Ladner and Yohe [26].

34. Griffith [27].

35. This section is based upon Ishikawa and San Miguel [31] and San Miguel and Ishikawa [32].

36. Moore, op. cit., pp. 3-4.

37. The method is to perform the same computation twice, carrying a greater number of significant figures in the arithmetic the second time, i.e., once in single precision and once in double precision. The number of figures to which the two calculations agree is supposed to reveal the accuracy of the first result.

38. Although some columns of the coefficient matrix may be reduced to zero when interval numbers are used in Gaussian Elimination, this difficulty can be

overcome through use of the Bisection Method. The Method locates real roots for a polynomial that has real coefficients. Letting $f(x)$ be a polynomial with real coefficients such that $f(a_1) \times f(a_2) < 0$ where c_1 and c_2 are are real numbers, the algorithm follows:

(1) Suppose $f(a_1) \times f(a_2) < 0$, with $a_1 < a_2$.
(2) Calculate $a_3 = (a_1 + a_2)/2$
   (a) If $f(a_3 < \epsilon$ for some positive ϵ, then a_3 is a root of $f(x)$.
   (b) If $f(a_3) \times f(a_1) < 0$, replace a_2 by a_3 and return to Step 2.
   (c) If $f(a_3) \times f(a_1) > 0$, replace a_1 by a_3 and return to Step 2.

The Bisection Method coverages, since for any $\epsilon > 0$, there exists a positive integer 'n' such that

$$(c_2 - c_1)/2^n < \epsilon$$

where n is the number of bisections.

39. See Moore [28], pp. 5-7.

40. Moore denotes the set of closed real intervals by l. Thus if $I \in l$, then $I = [a,b]$ for some real numbers a and b such that $a \leq b$.

41. Dwyer [29].

43. An assumption is made that endpoints are computed with infinite precision.

44. Moore, op. cit., p. 9.

45. Ibid.

46. Ibid., p. 10.

47. Ibid.

48. Ibid.

49. Burford [30].

50. Moore, op. cit., p. 10.

51. Ibid.

CHAPTER VI

Summary and Conclusions

Although there does exist a history relating to descriptive corporate planning and control models, not enough history exists for computerized corporate models.

As the socioeconomic system in which a corporation operates becomes more complex, management finds itself having to resort more and more to on-line decision making. This need emphasizes the importance of computerized corporate planning and control models as an ultimate objective in modeling development. These models can take care of routine operations which involve numerous replicating computations, but also can be extended to cover other managerial operations, with the objective of improving the quality of managerial decision making. Once this has been accomplished, these models can be directed toward dealing with confidential personnel planning and control, contingency planning and control, discovery of technological changes, and prediction of political climate and government policy, which requires an early warning or feedforward control. To meet these requirements, there is a need for continuous sensing of environmental factors, and this might even dictate a need for changes of objectives. If the objectives change,the strategic and the financial planning process (particularly the capital budgeting process) may be changed. All these changes may affect even routine operational control.

Ideally, it is desirable for a computerized corporate model to incorporate all of these requirements. It is unrealistic to expect design and construction of such a model. Each corporation should identify the parts of the whole corporate planning process to be computerized, and then evaluate the net benefit of such computerization at each stage of its development. Corporate models can contain both computerized and non-computerized corporate aspects.

RESTATEMENT OF THE SPECIFIC OBJECTIVES OF THIS STUDY

1. It was the objective of this text to provide a background and instructions

for the general approach to developing corporate planning and control models.

2. Identify the main problems involved in the development of corporate planning and control models, and to suggest solutions to these problems.

3. Suggest approaches to the solution of a number of specific problems which existing models do not appear to have solved. The problems studied were identification of user information requireements, provision of a basis for validating models, and application of management science techniques.

SUMMARY OF METHODOLOGY, FINDINGS, AND CONCLUSIONS

Basic Corporate Model-Development Problems and Solutions

The first and the second objective was accomplished by undertaking a thorough comparative analysis of modeling and modeling-related research efforts to date. This analysis included reference to the research efforts of the author, which have concerned the development of financial planning and control models for private and public organizations.

Study, Evaluation and Development of Corporate Models

The first step in the comparative analysis was an identification and explanation of the matters that require attention when studying, evaluating, and developing corporate models (Chapter II). Seven aspects of corporate models were identified: objectives, scope, design methods, users and uses, information requirements, data management, and management science techniques.

Under "objectives," it was indicated that corporate goals can be examined in terms of objective-setting (establishment of objectives) objective execution, and objectives improvement or refinement. Particular attention was given to the need for a definitive statement of the objectives.

Under "scope," approaches to scope-setting, evaluation and revision were introduced. An operations-oriented approach entails the use of corporate models on a certain operation or operations; accounting, finance, marketing, and personnel. A timing-oriented approach entails the use of corporate models on a timing basis rather than on an operation. It should be recognized that these approaches can be examined simultaneously in order to arrive at a more appropriate scope of the corporate model.

Three "design methods" (top-down, bottom-up, and eclectic) were discussed. The top-down approach places a higher priority on the information requirements of top management than on those of middle or lower management in designing, constructing, and refining the corporate model. The bottom-up approach places a higher priority on departmental or divisional application of the model than on structure and application to the corporation as a whole. The eclectic approach includes both the top-down and bottom-up. It was indicated that through the appropriate introduction of the eclectic approach the information requirements gap is alleviated, unnecessary details are avoided, and allocation of human, material, and information resources is made more efficiently.

Under "users and uses," users of corporate models were divided into three classes: corporate executives and divisional or departmental managers, specialists in planning, finance, and accounting, and students (potential executives, managers, or specialists). Users take initiatives at each of the important stages of model development. To increase the use of corporate models, communications to and from an executive or an ultimate user of the model are vitally important. Some sort of monitoring or appraisal system is required to follow up and continuously analyze the user-generated, analyst-generated, and system-generated estimates. The user objectives should be explained in terms of the purpose of the output. Who is to use the output and in what form (raw or analyzed)?

Much emphasis was placed on "inforamtion requirements." If the most important information requirements can be identified, the chances of constructing a successful model are high.

"Data management" encompasses many tasks. These include data collection, data processing, data retrieval, and data utilization. Data collection management entails collecting data that are quantitatively sufficient, qualitatively reliable, and helpful for decision making. Data processing management embraces all management of data processing functions and systems related to computers and software systems. Data retrieval management entails acquisition of relevant data whenever required. Therefore, the data retrieval function is dependent on enough data being collected, appropriate data processing, and specifically-stated retrieval requirements. Data utilization management is a follow-up management of data generation. It entails ascertaining how effectively-generated data are to be used. To realize successful data management, all of the important data management functions aforementioned should be identified, relationships of functions clarified, and continuous evaluations made on each function, as well as the data management system as a whole.

"Management science techniques" embrace all scientific techniques for corporate planning and control. Although most existing models are of the simulation type (according to Gershefski's survey)[1] it is expected that techniques such as mathematical programming for optimization models will be used more in the future. It is also not unlikely that new management science techniques will appear, as the development of corporate models is extended.

Model Construction Process

An outline of the process of constructing a model constituted the second part of the comparative analysis (Chapter III). Three key considerations were discussed: (1) the need for exchanging information through questionnaires, (2) timely adjustments to meet corporate policy changes during model development, and (3) thorough coordination among model users, model builders, and their representatives, if any. Four significant advantages of the questionnaire-response system were indicated: (1) investigation of key characteristics and requirements can be systematic, (2) any changes in the user's requirements can be anticipated, (3) differences of opinion among model users can be resolved, and

(4) priorities can be identified according to the degree of detail and order. The necessity of identifying priorities was stressed, and the priority matrix was introduced as a tool of identifying priorities. It was indicated that timely adjustment of the model to meet policy changes can only be achieved through adequate anticipation by the task force of modeling development. Three general guidelines for avoiding unnecessary delays caused by policy changes are: (1) continuous investigation of the environmental factors; (2) continuous understanding of the key issues in the company; and (3) continuous communication with an authoritative member of the user group. The coordination problem was divided into two categories: structural coordination and process coordination. While structural coordination is a planning coordination in nature that relies on the organizatonal hierarchy, process coordination entails follow-up coordination that should be dynamic on a time basis. It should be emphasized that from a practical point of view, structural and process coordination should be effected simultaneously in order to plan and control coordination in total.

In building FORPLANCON, and other models seven steps of model development were identified (they are summarized in Chapter III). These steps may not occur in the stated order. Particular emphasis was given to identification of information requirements (the third step). Inherent in the decision maker's authority is the responsibility to guide his subordinates by elucidating his preferences, as well as possible. There are three alternatives available for the step relating to the revision and expansion of a model: (1) gradual expansion and improvement, (2) discrete expansion into a corporate basis, and (3) decentralization. Requirements of the model must be continuously explored and examined. Saving of time and cost can be achieved in cases where a substantial change of requirements is inevitable.

Benefits to be Deirved from Corporate Models

The third and final step in the comparative analysis attempted to clarify exactly what corporate executives can expect from corporate models, and outlined specific considerations for ensuring acquisition of expected benefits (Chapter IV). Consequently, the user's needs must be clearly defined when the model is constructed. The benefits of the model are relative to the reliability, useability, predictability, and suggestibility of its output.

A model enables a model user to make deeper analyses, evaluate the soundness of planning, and make more confident judgments. The discussion on the ways of ensuring acquisition of such benefits focused on some of the system selection problems: (1) selection of either an existing manual or time-sharing system, and (2) selection of the best time-sharing system provided that a time-sharing system is to be chosen. Various factors to be taken into consideration in a cost-benefit study were identified. Three additional factors, training, reliability, and the relationship of a new system with the presently available system, were taken into consideration. To find the best system, model users and builders need to define the important factors, collect the necessary data, establish an appropriate model, and evaluate the alternatives. The decision to select a new system should be consistent with long-term system development planning and programmming.

MORE COMPLEX PROBLEMS AND SUGGESTED SOLUTIONS

The third objective was accomplished by describing approaches used by the author and others in practice (*a* and *b* of the third objective), and by describing a few important, relatively new techniques which, as a result of work on an actual model and other research, the author believes have significant application potential (*c* of the third objective).

User Information Requirements and Model Validation[2]

The user information requirements problem was covered as an integral part of the discussions of chapters II to IV, and in Chapter V the solution process is identified by the priority matrix and interval analysis techniques. The development of a basis for validating a model was covered as an integral part of chapters II and IV, and with reference to the interval analysis technique suggested in Chapter V. The development of a model is greatly facilitated when its information requirements and the basis of validation of its results are known.

The information-requirements problem relates to both inputs and outputs. There is a need to satisfy both information input and output requirements. Information output requirements, e.g., actual performance, should not deviate significantly from the anticipated figures. If upper and lower limits can be developed for the anticipated figures, validation, of the information requirements is facilitated because of the fact that actual figures (generated by the model as outputs) must then fall somewhere between these two limits.

Unexpected outputs (actual performance) produced by the model are likely to be the result of input or processing malfunctions. Input validation is geared to an evaluation as to whether input is free from bias, generated from the correct source at the correct time, and for the correct use. Functioning validation is geared to an evaluation as to whether the model is appropriately constructed.

To validate the model, ideally, a model validation model (a model of the model) is required. Such validation can be undertaken on the basis of an evaluation of the model's reliability, predictability, useability and suggestibility. (See discussion in the above section.)

Application of Management Science Techniques

Three management science concept and techniques were discussed in Chapter V. Among many other concepts and techniques the feedforward concept, priority matrix, and interval analysis were introduced in this text. This application and potential extensions were also discussed.

Feedforward planning and control is defined as anticipatory planning and control, in which preventive action is taken before the difference between planned and actual performance occurs. In order to explain the more specific role of feedforward control in an organizational planning and control system, it was differentiated from other control concepts. The application of the feedforward concept in management processes was highlighted, and an evaluation of feedforward's application potential made. This concept needs to be explored further in order to develop the specific techniques that will increase application possibilities.

The priority matrix was introduced as a means of clarifying a decision maker's preference and decision making mechanism. It is defined as a matrix which indicates specific user-priority requirements of each information element or financial item. It is, therefore, a representation of a user's decision mechanism (including his preferences), and all conceivable functional relationships between dependent and independent variables. The author's experience with such a matrix was illustrated, and variations from the original form were discussed. The priority matrix can be applied to planning and control decisions alone or, often, in conjunction with a decision diagram or decision tree.

Interval analysis has application potential as an intermediate means of analysis as well as an input and output representation which can cement the gap between a point estimate and a stochastic representation.

In addition to these three conceptual techniques, there are new computer languages, more useful programming techniques, more flexible file management techniques, hardware engineering techniques (such as more flexible, rapid access storage devices, more rapid input and output devices), and a hardware technique capable of implementing relatively large arrays of parallel data processing unit, to name a few, to be further explored.

THE DIRECTION OF FUTURE RESEARCH

In Chapter IV, the concepts of reliability, predictability, useability, and suggestibility were proposed as criteria for evaluating the contribution on specific models. Future research efforts should be directed toward improving the performance of corporate models on these four dimensions. It is the author's judgment that this can be accomplished by devoting specific efforts toward the design and construction of models that can adapt to changing external and internal factors.

Computerization of models facilitates incorporation of self-regulatory abilities. It would be helpful if such abilities included the ability to:

1. Initiate action to revise goals.
2. Initiate action to accomplish the revised goals.
3. Predict foreseeable important changes.

Existing models do not possess these abilities. A significant contribution can be made by developing this capability.

The information requirements problem has paramount relevance for this general area of research. It is suggested that the self-regulatory capacity of models can be developed by:

1. Identifying generalized as well as specific information requirements.

2. Developing for the model an appropriate degree of flexibility for coping with changing environmental conditions.[3]

This author was able to suggest methods for overcoming certain aspects of the problem. It is the author's belief that computer simulation models will never be successful unless information requirements are firmly identified. The lack of appropriate efforts in this direction is undoubtedly one of the reasons for some of the lawsuits against computer service companies. Users of these companies' models have complained that the models do not meet the requirements identified at the time of entering into the service contract.[4] It is clear that continuous research efforts are required in this area.

The second point (flexibility development) can be subdivided as follows:

1. Development of model flexibility for mathematical, logical, or behavioral models, etc.[5]
2. Model flexibility from a system engineering and programming standpoint.[6]
3. Model flexibility from the standpoint of contingency planning and control.

All the above are concerned with model development and organization to facilitate application by users or to assure maximum efficiency and adequacy of computers. After a routine planning and control model has been established, a contingency planning and control model would be a natural concern of many corporations. This contengency model would be based on emergency and/or low probability outcomes. It would be constrained to the extent that contingency information is available. Contingency information can be identified in terms of the nature of, and possible effect on, the corporate planning and control activities. In other words, it should be related to the continuity of the corporation.

Faced with an energy shortage, unemployment, population explosion, and increased interdependence, on top of inflation and recession, many corporations (organizations) will be increasingly required to foresee and measure that seemingly immeasurable. Computerized corporate planning and control models and systems would have to be so designed and constructed to cope with the contingencies we might possibly have more often than not in the future and provide the tools to understand our environment and predict ways to control that as much as possible.

The establishment of more homeostatic and synergetic corporate model systems, in which a set of models flexibly and pertinently function, responding to diversified information requirements, the design of intelligent, very large data bases, and internationalization of corporate models, are some of the solutions to cope with the incessantly changing world.

The more homeostatically designed corporate systems[7] should have sensing and self-organizing functions so that they may provide solutions to specific and one-time problems as well as routine and periodic ones serially and/or simultaneously. Cost effectiveness analysis may need to justify adding specific functions to the model systems.

The increasing on-line use of corporate models and the emerging design and development of large-scale storage devices ($10^{12} - 10^{15}$ bits and more) in a complex environment will necessitate both model builders and users to ·be oriented toward challenging with more intelligent management of very large data bases. This can provide the foundation, on which the model systems may best function.

The internationalization of corporate models[8] will also be more required, as we should be more concerned with the allocation policies and methods of limited resources on the earth with the increasing number and growth of multinational corporations.

There is one final area of research not referred to in this text. It concerns the development of a national (or a global[9]) model which could be constructed on the basis of models for all identifiable industries. The development of common frameworks for industry models by government, universities or industrial associations, for example, would facilitate the incorporation of individual corporate models. The essential objective of such a system of models would be to accomplish well-balanced growth of an individual company, and the economy as a whole. Because this implies a conscious effort at self-regulation of a whole economy, it might be possible to include more appropriate factors in the individual corporate models. Apart from the "how to do it" problem, decisions would have to be made as to who would control the industry and national models. But, whoever controls their future development and application, it is clear that corporate models will have significant impact on the evolution of the social and economic structure of all major, industrialized nations.

SUPPLEMENTARY READINGS

1. Barnett, C.C., Jr., and Associates. *The Future of Computer Utility*. New York: American Management Association, 1967.
2. Conference Board. *Information Technology: Some Critical Implications for Decision Making*. New York: Conference Board, 1972.
3. McLeavy, D. and Nobbs, A. "Corporate Planning Models: What Level of Futurity?" Proceedings of 1973 Northeast AIDS Conference, 429-434.
4. Salancik, G.R. *On the Nature of Economic Losses Arising from Computer-Based Systems in the Next Fifteen Years*. Menlo Park: California, the Institute for the Future, 1973.
5. Turn, R. *Air Force Command and Control Information Processing in the 1980's: Trend in Hardware Technology*, Rand Corporation R-1011-PR, October, 1972.

REVIEW QUESTIONS AND PROBLEMS

1. How do you foresee the future state of organizational (corporate) planning and control models?

2. What efforts should be directed toward improving the performance of corporate models?

3. If you were to attempt to incorporate self-regulatory abilities into computerized planning and control models, what specific abilities do you want to be included?

4. From the viewpoint of information requirements, what abilities should be incorporated into computer-based corporate models in the future?

5. From the viewpoint of model flexibility, what abilities should be incorporated into computerized corporate models in the future?

6. What should be basic considerations in establishing contingency planning models in the near future?

7. What would be a desirable relationship between a national (or global) model and a corporate model?

8. What should be key concerns in the development of industrial models by government or industrial associations. How should they relate to corporate planning and control models already developed by various corporations?

*9. What basic framework and methods would you propose to enable corporate models to make an impact on the evolution of the social and economic structures of major industrialized nations?

10. In what way can organizational planning and control models serve to enhance the social responsibility of each organization?

NOTES

1. See Gershefski [1], p. 41.

2. See also discussion under the next section.

3. This means that, on the one hand, the internal structure of the model or model system should be flexible, and that a selection process of the most relevant model in response to requirements should be highly intelligent. A much more expanded version of e.g., a general- and special-purpose optimum seeking program maybe required.

4. For further details of lawsuit cases, for example, see *The Wall Street Journal*, Nov. 30, 1970, p. 1.

5. The problem of organizing and storing various mathematical, logical, pictorial, and conceptual models in managerial planning, organizing, and controlling is discussed in Ishikawa [2], [3], [4], [5], [6], [7], [8], and Ansari, Ishikawa, and Smith [15].

6. Structured programming techniques may help develop the model flexibility on this point.

7. Generally stated, a well-balanced development of hardware (including the data transmission devices), software, and applicationnaire seems most important in developing those kinds of model systems.

8. For the implications of multinational computers and a simulation model for the multinational firm, see, for example, Nanus and Wooton [9], Nanus [10], and Fourcans and Hindelang [11], respectively.

9. Efforts have been made by Forrester [12] and Meadows [13] to design and construct global models and evaluate world problems. It is ideal if these models

were utilized by international leaders continuously as one of the vehicles for avoiding potential international conflicts, establishing better international policies for food and energy production and consumption, and for population, raw material consumption, natural conservation and land development, and allocating more equitably scarce resources. So are the cases with national and inter-industry (intercorporation) models. Ishikawa suggests the use of the models in the framework of Intellectual Olympics [14], that might be a means of expecting a sound model development on an international basis.

BIBLIOGRAPHY

CHAPTER I

1. Barnett, J. H. "Informative Systems: Overcoming the Barriers to Successful Utilization," *Management Review*, September 1969, pp. 9-14.
2. Gershefski, George W. "Building a Corporate Financial Model," *The Harvard Business Review*, 47 (July-August, 1969), pp. 61-72.
3. ———. The Development and Application of a Corporate Financial Model. Ohio: The Planning Executives Institute, 1968.
4. Naylor, Thomas H., ed. The Design of Computer Simulation Experiments. Durham, N.C.: Duke University Press, 1969.
5. Doenges, R. Conrad, Summers, Edward L., and Tavis, Lee A. Corporate Planning Models, Papers and Proceedings of The University of Texas Graduate School of Business Administration Corporate Planning Models Conference. Graduate School of Business, The University of Texas at Austin, November 24-25, 1969.
6. Schrieber, Albert N., ed. Corporate Simulation Models. Seattle, Washington: the University of Washington, 1970.
7. Seitz, Cameron W., "The Use of Long-Range, Interindustry Forecasting for Diversification Planning." Presented at the Chemical Marketing and Economic Section of the American Chemical Society Input/Output Meeting, September 11, 1967.
8. Boulden, James B. "Instant Modeling." Presented at the Symposium on Corporate Planning Models, the University of Washington, March 23-25, 1970.
9. Wagle, B. "The Use of Models for Environmental Forecasting and Corporate Planning," *Operational Research Quarterly*, 20, No. 3 (September, 1969), pp. 327-36.
10. Miller, Irvin M. "Computer Graphics for Decision Making," *The Harvard Business Review,* 47 (November-December, 1969), pp. 121-32.
11. Shostack, Kenneth, and Eddy, Charles. "Management by Computer Graphics," *The Harvard Business Review*, 49 (November-December, 1971), pp. 52-63.

12. Hamilton, William F., and Moses, Michael A. "A Computer-Based Corporate Planning System," *Management Science*, Vol. 12, No. 2 (October, 1974). pp. 148-59.

13. Murdick, Robert G., and Ross, Joel E. *Information Systems for Modern Management*. Englewood Cliffs, N.J.: Prentice-Hall, Inc., 1971.

CHAPTER II

1. Gershefski, George W. "Building a Corporate Financial Model," *The Harvard Business Review*, 47 (July-August, 1969), pp. 61-72.

2. _____ . "Corporate Models—The State of the Art." Presented at the Symposium on Corporate Simulation Models, the University of Washington, March 23-25, 1970.

3. Kohlmeier, John M. "A Framework for the Analysis of Corporate Models." Presented at the Corporate Planning Model Conference, The University of Texas at Austin, November 24-25, 1969.

4. Grens, Thomas B., Grad, Burton, Holstein, David, Meyers, William E., and Schmidt, Richard N. *Management Systems*. New York: Holt, Rinehart and Winston, Inc., 1968.

5. Murray, Gordon L. A 1970-Model Planning, Control, and Information System. New York: Haskins and Sells, 1969.

6. Gershefski, George W. "Planning—Models and People." Proceedings of the Symposium on Corporate Simulation Models, The Institute of Management Sciences, Seattle, Washington, March, 1970.

7. Kast, Fremont E., and Rosenzweig, James E. *Organization and Management: A System Approach*. New York: McGraw-Hill, 1970.

8. Caplan, Edwin H. *Management Accounting and Behavioral Science*. Reading, Mass.: Addison-Wesley Publishing Co., 1971.

9. Ishikawa, Akira. Cost-Effectiveness Analysis: Its Development, Present Status, and Potential Applications. Unpublished Thesis, the University of Washington, June, 1969.

10. Simon, Herbert A. *Administrative Behavior*. 2nd ed., New York: Macmillan Co., 1957.

11. Ishikawa, Akira. "The Development of a Corporate Financial Model: A Case Study." The Proceedings of the Accounting Colloquium of the Graduate School of Business, The University of Texas at Austin, 1971.

12. Jaffe, J. "The System Design phase," ed. by Perry E. Rosove, *Developing Computer-Based Information Systems*. New York: John Wiley & Sons, Inc., 1968.

13. Shaw, John C., and Atkins, William. *Managing Computer System Projects*. New York: McGraw-Hill, 1970.

14. Abe, Donald K. "Corporate Model Systems," ed. by Albert N. Schrieber, *Corporate Simulation Models*. Seattle: the University of Washington, 1970.

15. Brown, David E., and Redwood, Peter H. S. "The Xerox Planning Model."

Presented at the Corporate Planning Model Conference, The University of Texas at Austin, Nov. 24-25, 1969.

16. Chambers, John C., Mullick, Satinder K., and Smith, Donald D. "The Use of Simulation Models at Corning Glass Works," ed. Albert N. Schrieber, *Corporate Simulation Models*. Seattle: the University of Washington, 1970.

17. Fraser, John C. "A Corporate Model of a Large Mutual Life Insurance Co.," Presented at the Symposium on Corporate Simulation Models, Seattle, the University of Washington., Mar. 23-25, 1970 (New York Life Insurance Company).

18. Freeman, Gaylord A., Jr. "The Role Top Management must play in MIS Planning and Implementation." Proceedings of Founders' Conference of the Society for MIS, the University of Minnesota, Minneapolis, September 8-9, 1969.

19. Ayers, F. T., Kroeger, J. W., and Moseley, R. H. "Company Model Description for Corporate Planning Model Conference (Lockheed-Georgia Co.)." Presented at the Corporate Planning Model Conference, The University of Texas at Austin, Nov. 24-25, 1969.

20. Lastavica, John. "Financial Statement Analysis and the Projections on Time-Sharing Computers at the First National Bank of Boston." Presented at Corporate Planning Model Conference, The University of Texas at Austin, November 24-25, 1969.

21. Brandt, Hugh J. W., and Psozgai, Dale G. "The Strategic Planning System of Owens-Illinois, Inc." Presented at Corporate Planning Model Conference at The University of Texas at Austin, November 24-25, 1969.

22. Wagner, Wayne H., Akutagawa, Lawrence T., and Cunco, Larry J. "Telecommunications Earnings Estimation Model (TEEM): An Evaluation," ed. A. Schrieber, *Corporate Simulation Models*. Seattle: the University of Washington, 1970.

23. Dyment, John J. "Financial Planning with a Computer," *Financial Executive*, 28, No. 4 (April, 1970), p. 4.

24. Schrieber, Albert N., ed. *Corporate Simulation Models*. Seattle: the University of Washington, 1970.

25. Pryor, LeRoy J. "Simulation: Budgeting for a 'What If . . .'," *The Journal of Accountancy*, 130 (November, 1970) p. 60.

26. Khoury, E. N., and Nelson, H. Wayne. "Simulation in Financial Planning," *Management Services*, 2, No. 2(March-April, 1965), pp. 13-21.

27. Smith, J. L. "An Analysis of Time-Sharing Computer Systems Using Markov Models." Proc. AFIPS, Spring Joint Computer Conference, 28 (1966), pp. 87-95.

28. Robuck, Joel H. "RCA Information Systems Division Business Planning Model." Presented at Corporate Planning Model Conference, The University of Texas at Austin, November 24-25, 1969.

29. Ishikawa, Akira. "The Place of Management Information Systems in Developing the Planning, Programming and Budgeting System (PPBS)." Pre-

sented at the 5th International Operations Research Societies Conference, Venice, Italy, June, 1969.

30. Ishikawa, Akira, and Smith, Charles H. "Feedforward Control in the Total Planning and Control System," *Cost and Management*, Nov-Dec., 1972.

31. Struve, Donald L. "Corporate Models at American Airlines." Presented at the Corporate Planning Model Conference, The University of Texas at Austin, November 24-25, 1969.

32. Kibbec, Joel M., Craft, Clifford J., and Nanus, Burt. *Management Games*. New York: Reinhold Publishing Corporation, 1961.

33. Gray, Max, and London, Keith R. *Documentation Standards*. Princeton: Brandon/Systems Press, Inc., 1970, 5th printing.

34. Cohen, Kalman J., Dill, William R., Kuehn, Alfred A., and Winters, Peter R. *The Carnegie Tech Management Game: An Experiment in Business Education*. Homewood, Ill.: R. D. Irwin, 1964.

35. Rehg, Virgil R. "Simulation Model for Corporate Training Programs—Quality Control." Presented at the Symposium on Corporate Simulation Models, the University of Washington, March 23-25, 1970.

36. Goldie, J. Harry. "Simulation and Irritation." Presented at the Symposium on Corporate Simulation Models, the University of Washington, March 23-25, 1970.

37. Ackoff, Russell L. *A Concept of Corporate Planning*. New York: Wiley-Interscience, 1970.

38. Doenges, R. Conrad, Summers, Edward L., and Tavis, Lee A. Corporate Planning Models. Papers and Proceedings of The University of Texas Graduate School of Business Administration Corporate Planning Models Conference. Graduate School of Business, The University of Texas at Austin, November 24-25, 1969.

39. Bonner & Moore Associates, Inc. "Systems FP/70." Presented at the Corporate Planning Model Conference, The University of Texas at Austin, November 24-25, 1969.

40. Ishikawa, Akira. "Urban Problems and System Analysis (I)," *Urban Problems* (Japan), 58, No. 11 (1967).

41. _____ . "Urban Problems and Systems Analysis (II)," *Urban Problems*, 58, No. 12 (1967).

42. _____ . "Industrial Problems and System Engineering (I)," *Industrial Engineering* (Japan), November, 1967.

43. _____ . "Industrial Problems and System Engineering (II)," *Industrial Engineering*, November, 1967.

44. _____ . "Industrial Problems and System Engineering (III)," *Industrial Engineering*, January, 1968.

45. Reitman, Julian, Ingerman, Donald, Katzke, Jerry, Shapiro, Jon, Simon, Kenneth, and Smith, Burton. "A Complete Interactive Simulation Environment GRSS/360-NORDEN." Presented at the 4th Conference on Application of Simulation, Waldorf-Astoria Hotel, New York, December 9-11, 1970.

46. Shemer, Jack E. "Simulation and Mathematical Modeling of An On-Line Accounting System." Presented at the 4th Conference on Application of Simulation, Waldorf-Astoria Hotel, New York, December 9-11, 1970.

47. Dickson, G. W., Mauriel, J. J., and Anderson, J. C. "Computer Assisted Planning Models. A Functional Analysis," published in Schrieber, A. N., *Corporate Simulation Models*. Seattle: the University of Washington, 1970.

48. Grinyer, Peter H., and Batt, Christopher D. "Some Tentative Findings in Corporate Financial Simulation Models," *Operational Research Quarterly*, Vol. 25, No. 1 (March, 1974), pp.149-67.

49. Naylor, Thomas H., and Finger, J. M. "Verification of Computer Simulation Models," *Management Science*, Vol. 14, No. 2 (October, 1967), pp. B-92-B-101.

50. Ignall, Edward J., Kolesar, Peter, and Walker, Warren E. "The Use of Simulation in the Development and Empirical Validation of the Analytical Models for Emergency Services," The Proceedings of the 1974 Winter Simulation Conference, pp. 528-36.

51. Ishikawa, Akira, Carson, William, Eames, Morgan, and Huang, George. "A Pseudo-Language: A New Vehicle for Corporate Planning," Working Paper 74-87, Graduate School of Business Administration, College of Business and Public Administration, New York University, November, 1974.

52. Meadow, Charles T. *The Analysis of Information Systems*. Los Angeles, Calif.: Melville Publishing Co., 1973.

CHAPTER III

1. Ishikawa, Akira. "The Development of a Corporate Financial Model: A Case Study." Presented at the Accounting Colloquium of the Graduate School of Business, The University of Texas at Austin, December, 1970, and at the Accounting Workshop at the University of Chicago, January, 1971.

2. Prince, Thomas R. *Information Systems for Management Planning and Control*. Homewood, Illinois: Richard D. Irwin, Inc., 1970.

3. Dearden, John, McFarlan, F. Warren, and Zani, William M. *Managing Computer-Based Information Systems*. Homewood, Illinois: Richard D. Irwin, Inc., 1971.

4. Townsend, Robert. *Up the Organization: How to Stop the Corporation from Shifting People and Strangling Profits*. Greenwich, Conn.: Fawcett Publications, Inc., 1970.

5. Hare, Van Court. *Systems Analysis: A Diagnostic Approach*. New York: Harcourt Brace and World, 1967.

6. Raiffa, Howard. *Decision Analysis: Introductory Lectures on Choices Under Uncertainty*. Reading, Mass.: Addison-Wesley, 1970.

7. Pryor, LeRoy J. "Simulation: Budgeting for a 'What If . . .'," *The Journal of Accountancy*, 130 (November, 1970), p. 60.

8. Rappaport, Alfred. "Sensitivity Analysis in Decision Making," *Accounting Review*, 42 (July, 1967), pp. 441-56.

9. Greenberg, Joel S. "A Corporate Planning Model for a New Business Venture." Presented at 1971 Winter Simulation Conference (Fifth Conference on Application of Simulation), New York, December 8-10, 1971.
10. Jensen, Robert E. "JENCAT Extensions: Prediction Models and Multivariate Analysis of Variance in Terms of Prediction Error," *A Working Paper 72-10*, College of Business Administration, The University of Texas at Austin.
11. Fraser, John C. "A Corporate Model of a Large Mutual Life Insurance Co." Presented at the Symposium on Corporate Simulation Models, the University of Washington, March 23-25, 1970 (New York Life Insurance Company).
12. DesJardins, Robert B., and Lee, William B. "A Corporate Simulation Model and a Small Manufacturing Firm." Presented at the Symposium on Corporate Simulation Models, the University of Washington, March 23-25, 1970.
13. Struve, Donald L. "Corporate Models at American Airlines." Presented at the Corporate Planning Model Conference, The University of Texas at Austin, November 24-25, 1969.
14. Chervany, Norman L., Strom, John S., Boehlke, Ralph F. "An Operations Planning Model for the Northwestern National Bank of Minneapolis." Presented at the Symposium on Corporate Simulation Models, the University of Washington, March 23-25, 1970.
15. Boulden, James B. "Instant Modeling." Presented at the Symposium on Corporate Planning Models, the University of Washington, March 23-25, 1970 (On-Line Decisions, Inc.).
16. Ishikawa, Akira. "The Development of a Corporate Financial Model: A Case Study." The Proceedings of the Accounting Colloquium of the Graduate School of Business, The University of Texas at Austin, 1970-71.
17. Blumenthal, Sherman C. *Management Information Systems: A Framework for Planning and Development*. Englewood Cliffs, N.J.: Prentice-Hall, Inc. 1969.
18. Gershefski, George W. "Building a Corporate Financial Model," *The Harvard Business Review*, 47 (July-August, 1969), 61-72.
19. March, James G., and Simon, Herbert A. *Organizations*. New York: John Wiley and Sons, Inc., 1958.
20. Thompson, James D. *Organizations in Action*. New York: McGraw-Hill, 1967.
21. Boulding, Kenneth E. "A Pure Theory of Conflict Applied to Organizations," in George Fisk (ed.). *The Frontiers of Management Psychology*. New York: Harper & Row Publishers, Inc., 1964.
22. Barnard, Chester I. *The Functions of the Executives*. Cambridge, Mass.: Harvard University Press, 1938.
23. Head, Robert V. *Real-Time Business Systems*. New York: Holt, Rinehart and Winston, Inc., 1964.
24. Enke, Stephen (ed.), *Defense Management*. Englewood Cliffs, N.J.: Prentice-Hall, Inc., 1968, pp. 218-19.
25. Doenges, R. Conrad, Summers, Edward L., and Tavis, Lee A. Corporate Planning Models, Papers and Proceedings of The University of Texas Grad-

uate School of Business Administration Corporate Planning Models Conference. Graduate School of Business, The University of Texas at Austin, November 24-25, 1969.

26. Humble, John W. (ed.). *Management by Objectives in Action*. London: McGraw-Hill, 1970.

27. _____, "Management by Objectives," Occasional Paper Number Two, Industrial Education and Research Foundation, 1967.

28. Neuschel, Richard F. *Management by System*. New York: McGraw-Hill, 1960.

29. Stokes, Paul M. *A Total Systems Approach to Management Control*. New York: American Management Association, 1968.

30. Gershefski, George W. "Corporate Models—The State of the Art." Presented at the Symposium on Corporate Simulation Models, the University of Washington, March 23-25, 1970.

31. Sharpe, William F. *The Economics of Computers*. New York and London: Columbia University Press, 1969.

32. Scherr, Allan L. An Analysis of Time-Shared Computer Systems, doctoral thesis, Department of Electrical Engineering, M.I.T., June, 1965.

33. *Encyclopedia Dictionary of Systems and Procedures*. Prepared by the Prentice-Hall Editorial Staff. Englewood Cliffs, N.J.: Prentice-Hall, Inc., 1966.

34. Hibbs, R. F. "Dinner Address," at the 2nd Annual Conference of the Society of Management Information Systems. Washington, D.C.: Shoreham Hotel, September 14-15, 1970.

35. Burch, John G., Jr., and Strater, Felix R., Jr. *Information Systems: Theory and Practice*. Santa Barbara, California: Hamilton Publishing Co., 1974.

CHAPTER IV

1. Jensen, Robert E. "A Multiple Regression Model for Cost Control—Assumptions and Limitations," *The Accounting Review*, 41 (October, 1966), pp. 265-73.

2. Labovitz, Sanford I. "Criteria for Selecting a Significance Level: A Note on the Sacredness of .05." *American Sociologist*, 3 (1968), pp. 220-22.

3. Anthony, Robert N. *Planning and Control Systems: Framework for Analysis*. Cambridge: Harvard University Press, 1965.

4. O'Brien, James J. *Management Information Systems: Concepts, Techniques, and Applications*. New York: Van Nostrand-Reinhold Company, 1970.

5. McCormick, Ernest J. *Human Factors Engineering*. New York: McGraw-Hill, 1964.

6. Meister, David, and Rabideau, Gerald F. *Human Factors Evaluation in System Development*. New York: John Wiley & Sons, Inc., 1965.

7. Desmonde, William H. *A Controversial Graphic Data Processing System: The IBM 1130/2250*. Englewood Cliffs, N. J.: Prentice-Hall, Inc., 1969.

8. Green, R. Elliot, and Parslow, R. D., eds. *Computer Graphics in Management*. London: Gower Press, Limited, 1970.
9. Bright, James R., ed. *Technological Forecasting for Industry and Government: Methods and Applications*. Englewood Cliffs, N. J.: Prentice-Hall, Inc., 1968.
10. Sherwin, C. W., and Isenson, R. S. First Interim Report on Project HINDSIGHT, Office of the Director of Defense Research and Engineering, Clearing-House for Scientific and Technical Information No. AD 642-400, June 30, 1966, revised, October 13, 1966.
11. Jantsch, Erich. *Technological Forecasting in Perspective*. Paris: O. E. C. D., 1967.
12. ———, ed. *Perspectives of Planning*. Paris: O. E. C. D., 1969.
13. ———. *Technological Planning and Social Values*. N. Y.: John Wiley & Sons, Inc., 1972.
14. Schneeweiss, Christoph A. "Smoothing Production by Inventory—An Application of the Wiener Filtering Theory," *Management Science*, 17, No. 7 (March, 1971), pp. 472-83.
15. Schiff, Michael, and Lewin, Arie Y. *Behavioral Aspects of Accounting*. Englewood Cliffs, N. J.: Prentice-Hall, Inc., 1974.
16. Byrne, R.F., Charnes, A., Cooper, W.W., Davis, O.A., Gilford, Dorothy, eds., *Studies in Budgeting*. Amsterdam: North-Holland Publishing Co., 1971.
17. Theil, H. *Economic Forecasts and Policy*. Amsterdam: North-Holland Publishing Co., 1961.
18. ———. *Applied Economic Forecasting*. Chicago: Rand McNally, 1966.
19. Siegel, Sidney. *Nonparametric Statistics*. New York: McGraw-Hill, 1956.
20. Walsh, John E. *Handbook of Nonparametric Statistics I and II*. Princeton, N. J.: D. Van Nostrand Co., 1962, 1965.
21. Smith, L. F. *An Executive Briefing on the Control of Computers*, Park Ridge, Ill.: Data Processing Management Association, 1971.
22. Haidinger, Timothy P., and Richardson, Rick. *Manager's Guide to Computer Timesharing*. New York: Wiley-Interscience, 1975.

CHAPTER V

1. Shinskey, F. G. "Feedforward Control Applied," *ISA Journal*, November, 1963, pp. 61-5.
2. MacMullan, E. C., and Shinskey, F. G. "Feedforward Analog Computer Control of a Superfractionator," *Control Engineering*, March, 1964, pp. 69-74.
3. Luyben, W. L., and Gerster, J. A. "Feedforward Control of Distillation Columns," *Industrial and Engineering Chemistry Design and Development*, October, 1964, pp. 374-81.
4. Forrester, Jay W. *Industrial Dynamics*. Cambridge, Mass.: Technology Press, and New York: John Wiley & Sons, Inc., 1961.
5. American Institute of Electrical Engineers Committee Report. "Proposed

Symbols and Terms for Feedback Control Systems," *Electrical Engineering*, October, 1951.

6. Shinskey, F. G. *Process Control Systems*. New York: McGraw-Hill, 1967.

7. Koppel, Lowell B. *Introduction to Control Theory with Applications to Process Control*. Englewood Cliffs, New Jersey: Prentice-Hall, Inc., 1968.

8. Murphy, Roy E., Jr. *Adaptive Processes in Economic Systems*. New York: Academic Press, 1965.

9. McGuire, M. L. "Optimal Feedforward-Feedback Control of Dead Time Systems," *Industrial and Engineering Chemistry Fundamentals*, 8(May, 1969), pp. 253-57.

10. Haskins, D. E., and Sliepcevich, C. M. "Invariant Principle of Control for Chemical Processes," *Industrial and Chemistry Fundamentals*, 4(August, 1965), pp. 241-48.

11. Rappaport, Alfred. "Sensitivity Analysis in Decision Making," *The Accounting Review*, 42(July, 1967), pp. 441-56.

12. Jensen, Robert E. "Sensitivity Analysis and Integer Linear Programming," *The Accounting Review*, 43(July, 1968), pp. 425-46.

13. Hartley, Ronald V. "Some Extensions of Sensitivity Analysis," *The Accounting Review*, 45(April, 1970), pp. 223-34.

14. Benston, George J. "Multiple Regression Analysis of Cost Behavior," *The Accounting Review*, 41(October, 1966), pp. 657-72.

15. Brown, Robert Goodell. *Smoothing, Forecasting, and Prediction of Discrete Time Series*. Englewood Cliffs, New Jersey: Prentice-Hall, Inc., 1963.

16. Gross, Donald, and Ray, Jack L. "A General Purpose Forecasted Simulator," *Management Science*, 11, No. 6(April, 1965), pp. 119-35.

17. Batty, M. "Monitoring an Exponential Smoothing Forecasting System," *Operational Research Quarterly*, 20, No. 3(September, 1969), pp. 319-25.

18. Gabor, D., Wilby, W., and Woodcock, R. "A Universal Non-Linear Filter, Predictor, and Simulator Which Optimizes Itself by a Learning Process," Proceedings of the Inst. of Elect. Eng., 108-B, No. 40(1961), pp. 422-38.

19. Ivakhnenko, A. G., and Lapa, V. G. *Cybernetics and Forecasting Techniques*. New York: Elsevier, 1967.

20. Sunaga, T. "Theory of an Interval Algebra and Its Application to Numerical Analysis," RAAG Memoirs II, Tokyo: Gakujutsu Bunken Fukyu-Kai, 1958.

21. Fischer, P. C. "Automatic Propagated and Round-Off Error Analysis," presented at the 13th National Meeting of the ACM, Los Angeles, 1958.

22. Moore, R. E. "Automatic Error Analysis in Digital Computation," LMSD-48421, Lockheed Missiles and Space Co., Palo Alto, California, January, 1959.

23. Moore, Ramon E. *Interval Analysis*. Englewood Cliffs, New Jersey: Prentice-Hall, Inc., 1966.

24. Boche, R. E. "An Operational Interval Arithmetic." Presented at IEEE National Electronics Conference, Chicago, October, 1963.

25. Burford, Leslie Jeanne. "Interval Analysis and Applications," Master's Thesis, The University of Texas at Austin, August, 1968.

26. Ladner, Thomas D., and Yohe, J.M. "An Interval Arithmetic Package for the UNIVAC 1108." MRC Report No. 1055, May, 1970.
27. Griffith, Hugh Wallace. Preliminary Investigations Using Interval Arithmetic in the Numerical Evaluation of Polynomials. The University of Texas at Austin, Doctoral Dissertation, December, 1970.
28. See reference 23.
29. Dwyer, P. S. *Linear Computations*. New York: John Wiley & Sons, Inc., 1951.
30. See reference 25.
31. Ishikawa, Akira, and San Miguel, Joseph G. "The Use of Interval Estimates in Accounting Report," a Working Paper 73-15, Graduate School of Business Administration, New York Univ., February, 1973.
32. San Miguel, Joseph G., and Ishikawa, Akira. "The Use of Interval Estimates in Managerial Decision Models," HBS 75-3, Graduate School of Business Administration, Harvard University, January, 1975.
33. Lazzaro, V., ed. *Systems and Procedures: A Handbook for Business and Industry*. Englewood Cliffs, New Jersey: Prentice-Hall, 1968.
34. Maynard, H. B., ed. *Industrial Engineering Handbook*. New York: McGraw-Hill, 1971.
35. ——, ed. *Handbook of Business Administration*. New York: McGraw-Hill, 1967.
36. Hartman, W. et al. *Management Information Systems Handbook*. New York: McGraw-Hill, 1968.
37. Ishikawa, Akira, and Smith, Charles H. "A Feedforward Control System for Organizational Planning and Control," *Abacus*, Vol. 8, No. 2, 1972, pp. 163-80.
38. ——, "Feedforward Control in the Total Planning and Control System," *Cost and Management*, Vol. 46, No. 6, 1972, pp. 36-41.
39. Jenkins, G. M., and Watts, D. G. Spectral Analysis and Its Applications. San Francisco: Holden-Day, 1968.
40. Wheelwright, Steve C., and Makridakis, S. *Forecasting Methods for Management*. New York: John Wiley & Sons, 1973.
41. Social Systems, Inc. *SIMPLAN: Marketing*. Durham, N.C.: SSI, September, 1973.
42. Hoffman, Lance J. *Security and Privacy in Computer Systems*. Los Angeles, Calfiornia: Melville Publishing Co., 1973.
43. Allen, Brandt. "Danger Ahead! Safeguard Your Computer," *The Harvard Business Review*, Nov.-Dec., 1968, pp. 97-101.
44. Bates, William S. "Security of Computer-Based Information Systems," *Datamation*, May, 1970.
45. Nelson, Charles R. *Applied Time Series Analysis*. San Francisco, California: Holden-Day, Inc., 1973.
46. Machol, Robert E., ed. *System Engineering Handbook*. New York: McGraw-Hill, 1965.

47. Pearson, Carl E., ed. *Handbook of Applied Mathematics*. New York: Van Nostrand Reinhold, 1974.
48. Claire, William H. *Handbook on Urban Planning*. New York: Van Nostrand Reinhold, 1973.
49. Korn, Granino A., and Korn, Theresa M. *Mathematical Handbook for Scientists and Engineers*. New York: McGraw-Hill, 1968.
50. Keppel, Geoffrey. *Design and Analysis: A Researcher's Handbook*. Englewood Cliffs, New Jersey: Prentice-Hall, 1973.

CHAPTER VI

1. Gershefski, George W. "Planning—Models and People." Proceedings of the Symposium on Corporate Simulation Models, The Institute of Management Sciences, Seattle, Washington, March, 1970.
2. Ishikawa, Akira. "Urban Problems and System Analysis(I)," *Urban Problems (Japan)*, 58, No. 11, 1967.
3. _____. "Urban Problems and System Analysis(II)," *Urban Problems (Japan)*, 58, No. 12, 1967.
4. _____. "The Place of Management Information System (MIS) in Developing the PPBS (Planning, Programming, and Budgeting System)," Proceedings of the Fifth International Federation of Operations Research Societies. London and New York: Tavistock Publications, 1970, pp. 535-44.
5. _____. "The Development of a Corporate Financial Model: A Case Study." Presented at the Accounting Colloquium of the Graduate School of Business, The University of Texas at Austin, December, 1970; and at the University of Chicago, January, 1972.
6. _____. "Industrial Problems and System Engineering (I)," *Industrial Engineering (Japan)*, November, 1967.
7. _____. "Industrial Problems and System Engineering (II)," *Industrial Engineering (Japan)*, December, 1967.
8. _____. "Industrial Problems and System Engineering (III)," *Industrial Engineering (Japan)*, January, 1968.
9. Nanus, Burt, and Wooton, Michael Leland, "Implications of Multinational Computers," *Business Horizons*, February, 1974, pp. 5-17.
10. Nanus, Burt, "The Multinational Computer," *Columbia Journal of World Business*, IV, No. 6 (November-December), 1969, pp. 7-14.
11. Fourcans, Andre, and Hindelang, Thomas J. "Working Capital Management for the Multinational Firm: A Simulation Model," Proceedings of 1974 Winter Simulation Conference, pp. 141-49.
12. Forrester, Jay W. *World Dynamics*. Cambridge, Mass.: Wright-Allen Press, 1971.
13. Meadows, Donella H. et al. *The Limits to Growth* New York: Universe Books, 1972.

CORPORATE PLANNING AND CONTROL

14. Ishikawa, Akira, "The Framework of Intellectual Olympics," *Yushi* (Japan), Vol. 14, 1968.

15. Ansari, Shahid, Ishikawa, Akira, and Smith, Charles, "Behavioral Factors and the Design of Control Systems," a paper presented at *the Institute of Management Sciences XXII International Meeting*, held in Kyoto, Japan, July 23-26, 1975.

BIBLIOGRAPHY

BOOKS

1. Ackoff, Russell L. *A Concept of Corporate Planning*. New York: Wiley-Interscience, 1970.
2. Anthony, Robert N. *Planning and Control Systems: A Framework for Analysis*. Boston, Mass.: Harvard University Press, 1965.
3. Barnard, Chester I. *The Functions of the Executives*. Cambridge, Mass.: Harvard University Press, 1938.
4. Barnett, C. C., Jr., and Associates. *The Future of the Computer Utility*. New York: American Management Association, 1967.
5. Barton, R. F. *A Primer on Simulation and Gaming*. Englewood Cliffs, N. J.: Prentice-Hall, Inc. 1970.
6. Blumenthal, Sherman C. *Management Information Systems: A Framework for Planning and Development*. Englewood Cliffs, N. J.: Prentice-Hall, Inc., 1969.
7. Bright, James R., ed. *Technological Forecasting for Industry and Government: Methods and Applications*. Englewood Cliffs, N. J.: Prentice-Hall, Inc., 1968, pp. 35-54.
8. Brown, Robert Goodell. *Smoothing, Forecasting, and Prediction of Discrete Time Series.*. Englewood Cliffs, N. J.: Prentice-Hall, Inc., 1963.
9. Burch, John G., Jr. and Strater, Felix R., Jr. *Information Systems: Theory and Practice*. Santa Barbara, California: Hamilton Publishing Co., 1974.
10. Caplan, Edwin H. *Management Accounting and Behavioral Science*. Reading, Mass.: Addison-Wesley Publishing Co., 1971.
11. Churchill, Neil C., Kempster, John H., and Uretsky, Myron. *Computer-Based Information Systems for Management: A Survey*. New York: National Association of Accountants, 1969.
12. Cohen, Kalman J., Dill, William R., Kuehn, Alfred A., Winters, Peter R. *The Carnegie Tech Management Game: An Experiment in Business Education* Homewood, Ill.: R. D. Irwin, 1964.
13. Couger, J. Daniel, and Knapp, Robert W., eds. *System Analysis Techniques*. New York: John Wiley and Sons, 1974.

23. Humble, John W., ed. *Management by Objectives in Action*. London: McGraw-Hill, 1970.

24. Ivakhnenko, A. G., and Lapa, V. G. *Cybernetics and Forecasting Techniques*. New York: Elsevier, 1967.

25. Jantsch, Erich. *Technological Forecasting in Perspective*. Paris: O.E.C.D., 1967.

26. Jenkins, G. M. and Watts, D. G. (Chapter 5, 39)

27. Kast, Fremont E., and Rosenzweig, James E. *Organization and Management: A system Approach*. New York: McGraw-Hill, 1970.

28. Kelly, Joseph F. *Computerized Management Information Systems*. New York: The Macmillan Company, 1970.

29. Kibbec, Joel M., Craft, Clifford J., and Nanus, Burt. *Management Games*. New York: Reinhold Publishing Corporation, 1961.

30. Koppel, Lowell B. *Introduction to Control Theory with Applications to Process Control*. Englewood Cliffs, N.J.: Prentice-Hall, Inc., 1968.

31. Lazzaro, V. ed. (Chapter 5, 33).

32. Lucas, Henry C., Jr. *Computer Based Information Systems in Organizations*, Chicago: Science Research Associates, Inc., 1973.

33. Lucas, Henry C., Jr. (Chapter 4, SR, 5)

34. March, James C., and Simon, Herbert A. *Organizations*. New York: John Wiley and Sons, Inc., 1958.

35. Mathison, Stuart L., and Walker, Philip M. *Computers and Telecommunications*. Englewood Cliffs, N. J.: Prentice-Hall, Inc., 1970.

36. Maynard, H. B. (Chapter 5, 34, 35).

37. McCormick, Ernest J. *Human Factors Engineering*. New York: McGraw-Hill, 1964.

38. Meadow, Charles T. (Chapter 2, 52).

39. Meadows, D. H. (Chapter 6, 13).

40. Meister, David, and Rabideau, Gerald F. *Human Factors Evaluation in System Development*. New York: John Wiley and Sons, Inc., 1965.

41. Moore, Ramon E. *Interval Analysis*. Englewood Cliffs, N. J.: Prentice-Hall, Inc., 1966.

42. Murdick, Robert G., and Ross, Joel E. *Information Systems for Modern Management*, Englewood Cliffs, N. J.: Prentice-Hall, 1971.

43. Murphy, Roy E., Jr. *Adaptive Processes in Economic Systems*. New York: Academic Press, 1965.

44. Naylor, Thomas H. *Computer Simulation Experiments with Models of Economic Systems*. New York: John Wiley & Sons, Inc., 1971.

45. Neuschel, Richard F. *Management by System*. New York: McGraw-Hill, 1960.

REPORTS

46. Abe, Donald K. "Corporate Model System." Presented at the Symposium on

Corporate Simulation Models, the University of Washington, March 23-25, 1970 (Esso Mathematics and Systems, Inc.).

47. Aida, Shuichi. "IMICTRON Modulated Learning Control System." Presented at the 1st International Conference on System Sciences, Honolulu, Hawaii, January 29-31, 1968.

48. American Institute of Electrical Engineers Committee Report. "Proposed Symbols and Terms for Feedback Control Systems." *Electrical Engineering*, October, 1951.

49. Auerbach Corporation. Final Report, 1570-TR-1. Philadelphia, Pa.: Auerbach Corp., 1968.

50. Ayers, F. T., Kroeger, J. W., and Moseley, R. H. "Company Model Description for Corporate Planning Model Conference (Lockheed-Georgia Company)." Presented at the Corporate Planning Model Conference, The University of Texas at Austin, November 24-25, 1969.

51. Boche, R.E. "An Operational Internal Arithmetic." Presented at IEEE National Electronics Conference, Chicago, October, 1963.

52. Bonner & Moore Associates, Inc. "System FP/70." Presented at the Corporate Planning Model Conference, The University of Texas at Austin, November 24-25, 1969.

53. Boulden, James B. "Instant Modeling." Presented at the Symposium on Corporate Planning Models, the University of Washington, March 23-25, 1970 (On-Line Decisions, Inc.).

54. Brandt, Hugh J. W., and Poszgai, Dale G. "The Strategic Planning System of Owens-Illinois, Inc." Presented at the Corporate Planning Model Conference, The University of Texas at Austin, November 24-25, 1969.

55. Brown, David E., and Redwood, Peter H. S. "The Xerox Planning Model." Presented at the Corporate Planning Model Conference, The University of Texas at Austin, November 24-25, 1969.

56. Chambers, John C., Mullick, Satinder K., Smith, Donald D. "The Use of Simulation Models at Corning Glass Works." Presented at the Symposium on Corporate Simulation Models, the University of Washington, March 23-25, 1970.

57. Chervany, Norman L., Strom, John S., Boehlke, Ralph F. "An Operations Planning Model for the Northwestern National Bank of Minneapolis." Presented at the Symposium on Corporate Simulation Models, the University of Washington, March 23-25, 1970.

58. Coffman, Edward G., Jr., and Kleinrock, Leonard. "Computer Scheduling Methods and Their Countermeasures," Proc. AFIPS, Spring Joint Computer Conference, 32 (1968), pp. 11-21.

59. Coffman, E. G. Stochastic Models of Multiple and Time Shared Computer Operations. U.C.L.A., Dept. of Engineering, Report No. 66-38, June, 1966.

60. DesJardins, Robert B., and Lee, William B. "A Corporate Simulation Model and A Small Manufacturing Firm." Presented at the Symposium on Corporate Simulation Models, the University of Washington, March 23-25, 1970.

61. Dickson, G.W., Mauriel, J.J., and Anderson, J.C. (See Chapter 2, 47).

62. Doenges, R. Conrad, Summers, Edward L., and Tavis, Lee A. Corporate Planning Models, Papers and Proceedings of the University of Texas Graduate School of Business Administration Corporate Planning Models Conference. Graduate School of Business, The University of Texas at Austin, November 24-25, 1969.

63. Engberg, Robert E. and Moore, Roger L. "A Corporate Planning Model for a Construction Materials Producer." Presented a joint national meeting of The Institute of Management Sciences, Operations Research Society of America and American Institute of Industrial Engineers, Atlantic City, N.J., November 8-10, 1972.

64. Estrin, A., and Kleinrock, Leonard. "Measures, Models and Measurements for Time-Shared Computer Utilities," Proceedings of ACM 22nd National Conference, 1967, pp. 85-96.

65. Fife, Dennis W. "An Optimization Model for Time-Sharing," Proc. AFIPS, Spring Joint Computer Conference, 28 (1966), pp. 97-104.

66. Fischer, P. C. "Automatic Propagated and Round-Off Error Analysis." Presented at the 13th National Meeting of the A.C.M., Los Angeles, 1958.

67. Fourcans, Andre, and Hindelang, Thomas J. "Working Capital Management for the Multinational Firm: A Simulation Model." Proc. of 1974 Winter Simulation Conference, pp. 141-47.

68. Fraser, John C. "A Corporate Model of a Large Mutual Life Insurance Company." Presented at the Symposium on Corporate Simulation Models, the University of Washington, March 23-25, 1970 (New York Life Insurance Company).

69. Freedman, Lee A. "The Impact of Technology on the Future State of Information Technology Enterprise." 1973 AFIPS Conference Proceedings, vol. 42, pp. 751-57.

70. Freeman, Gaylord, A., Jr. "The Role Top Management must play in MIS Planning and Implementation." Proceedings of Founders' Conference of the Society for Management Information Systems, University of Minnesota, Minneapolis, September 8-9, 1969.

71. Gabor, D., Wilby, W., and Woodcock, R. "A Universal Non-Linear Filter, Predictor and Simulator Which Optimizes Itself by a Learning Process." Proceedings of the Institute of Electrical Engineers, 108-B, No. 40 (1961), pp. 422-38.

72. Gershefski, George W. "Corporate Models—The State of the Art." Presented at the Symposium on Corporate Simulation Models, the University of Washington, March 23-25, 1970.

73. _____. The Development and Application of a Corporate Financial Model. Ohio: The Planning Executives Institute, 1968.

74. _____. "Planning—Models and People." Proceedings of the Symposium on Corporate Simulation Models, The Institute of Management Sciences, Seattle, Washington, March, 1970.

75. Goldie, J. Harry. "Simulation and Irritation." Presented at the Symposium

on Corporate Simulation Models, the University of Washington, March 23-25, 1970.

76. Greenberg, Joel S. "A Corporate Planning Model for a New Business Venture." Presented at 1971 Winter Simulation Conference (Fifth Conference on Application of Simulation), New York, December 8-10, 1971.

77. Hoggatt, Austin Curwood, and Balderston, Frederick E. Symposium on Simulation Models: Methodology and Applications to the Behavioral Sciences. Cincinnati, Ohio: Southwestern Publishing Co., 1963.

78. Howard, Ronald. "Semi-Markovian Control System." Technical Report No. 3, Contract No. 1841 (87), Operations Research Center, MIT, Cambridge, Mass.

79. Humble, John W. "Management by Objectives." Occasional Paper Number Two, Industrial Educational and Research Foundation, 1967.

80. Ignall, Edward J., Kolesar, Peter, and Walker, Warren E. "The Use of Simulation in the Development and Empirical Validation of the Analytical Models for Emergency Services," The Proceedings of 1974 Winter Simulation Conference, pp. 528-36.

81. Ignall, Edward J. et al. (Chapter 2, 50).

82. Ishikawa, Akira. "The Place of Management Information Systems in Developing the Planning, Programming, and Budgeting System (PPBS)." Presented at the 5th International Operations Research Societies Conference, Venice, Italy, June, 1969.

83. _____, "The Development of a Corporate Financial Model: A Case Study." Presented at the Accounting Colloquium of the Graduate School of Business, The University of Texas at Austin, December, 1970. The Proceedings of the Accounting Colloquium, 1970-71.

84. _____, and Smith, Charles H. "A Feed-forward Control System for Organizational Planning and Control." Presented at the 40th Annual Conference of the Operations Research Society of America, Working Paper 71-53, Graduate School of Business, The University of Texas at Austin, June, 1971.

85. _____. "An Interactive Educational Planning Model," Presented at ORSA-TIMS-AIEE 1972 Joint National Meeting at Atlantic City, N. J., Nov. 8-10, 1972.

86. _____. "The Application of Interval Analysis to Corporate Planning and Control Models," Presented at the 20th International Meeting of The Institute of Management Sciences at Tel Aviv, Israel, June, 1973.

87. _____. "Benefits from Computerized Corporate Models and Ways of Acquiring Them," The Proceedings of the 13th Annual Technical Symposium, Washington, D.C., 1974.

88. Kay, R.H. (Chapter 4, SR, 4).

89. Kohlmeier, John M. (Arthur Anderson and Company). "A Framework for the Analysis of Corporate Models." Presented at the Corporate Planning Model Conference, The University of Texas at Austin, November 24-25, 1969.

90. Ladner, Thomas D., and Yohe, J. M. "An Internal Arithmetic Package for the UNIVAC 1108." MRC Report No. 1055, May, 1970.

91. Lastavica, John. "Financial Statement Analysis and the Projections on Time-sharing Computers at the First National Bank of Boston." Presented at the Corporate Planning Model Conference, The University of Texas at Austin, November 24-25, 1969.

92. McLeavey and Nobbs (Chapter 6, SR, 3).

93. Moore, R. E. "Automatic Error Analysis in Digital Computaton." LMSD-48421, Lockheed Missiles and Space Co., Palo Alto, California, January, 1959.

94. Murray, Gordon L. A 1970-Model Planning, Control, and Information System. New York: Haskins and Sells, 1969.

95. Murray, Oliver, and Ishikawa, Akira. "On Modulo-Argument and Its Applications, Working Paper 74-66, Graduate School of Business Administration, New York University, August, 1974.

96. Nanus, Burt, Wooton, Michael, and Berke, Harold. "The Social Implications of the Use of Computers across National Boundaries." 1973 AFIPS Conference Proceedings, Vol. 42, pp. 735-45.

97. Naylor, Thomas H., ed. The Design of Computer Simulation Experiments. Durham, N. C.: Duke University Press, 1969.

98. ———. The Politics of Corporate Model Building, Durham, N.C.: Social Systems, Inc., 1974.

99. Norby, William C. "The Need and Responsibilities of the Investor in Equities." Presented at the Symposium on Corporate Financial Reporting held in New Jersey at the Seaview County Club, November 7-8, 1968.

100. Rehg, Virgil R. "Simulation Model for Corporate Training Programs— Quality Control." Presented at the Symposium on Corporate Simulation Models, the University of Washington, March 23-25, 1970.

101. Reitman, Julian, Ingerman, Donald, Katzke, Jerry, Shapiro, Jon, Simon, Kenneth, and Smith, Burton. "A Complete Interactive Simulation Environment GRSS/360-NORDEN." Presented at the 4th Conference on Application of Simulation, Waldorf-Astoria, New York, December 9-11, 1970.

102. Robuck, Joel H. "RCA Information Systems Division Business Planning Model." Presented at' the Corporate Planning Model Conference, The University of Texas at Austin, November 24-25, 1969.

103. Salancik, G.R. (Chap. 6, SR, 4).

104. Schaffer, Robert H. Managing by Total Objectives (Management Bulletin No. 52), American Management Association, General Management Division, New York, 1964.

105. Schrieber, Albert N., ed. Corporate Simulation Models. Seattle, Wash.: the University of Washington, 1970.

106. Seitz, Cameron W. "The Use of Long-Range, Interindustry Forecasting for Diversification Planning." Presented at the Chemical Marketing and Economic Section of the American Chemical Society Input/Output Meeting, September 11, 1967.

107. Shemer, Jack E. "Simulation and Mathematical Modeling of An On-Line Accounting System." Presented at the 4th Conference on Application of Simulation, Waldorf-Astoria, New York, December 9-11, 1970.

108. Sherwin, C.W., and Isenson, R.S. First Interim Report on Project HIND-SIGHT, Office of the Director of Defense Research and Engineering, Clearinghouse for Scientific and Technical Information #AD 642-400, June 30, 1966, revised, October 13, 1966.

109. Sholl, Howard A. "Model of the Human in a Short-Term, Visual, Information-Processing Task." Proceedings of the 4th Annual Princeton Conference on Information Sciences and Systems, Princeton University, Princeton, N.J., 1970, pp. 48-49.

110. Shubik, Martin, and Brewer, Garry D. "Reviews of Selected Books and Articles on Gaming and Simulation," Rand Corporation, R-732-ARPA, June 1972.

111. Smith, James D. "Dayton Hudson Corporation Financial Planning Models." Presented at the Corporate Planning Model Conference at the University of Texas at Austin, November 24-25, 1969.

112. Smith, J.L. "An Analysis of Time-Sharing Computer Systems Using Markov Models." Proc. AFIPS, Spring Joint Computer Conference, 28 (1966), pp. 87-95.

113. Struve, Donald L. "Corporate Models at American Airlines." Presented at the Corporate Planning Model Conference, The University of Texas at Austin, November 24-25, 1969.

114. Social Systems, Inc. (Chapter 5, 41).

115. Sunaga, T. "Theory of an Interval Algebra and Its Application to Numerical Analysis." RAAG Memoirs II, Tokyo: Gakujutsu Bunken Fukyu-kai, 1958.

116. Turn, R. (Chap. 6, SR, 5).

PAPERS

117. Allen, Brandt (Chapter 4, 43).

118. Barnett, J. H., "Information Systems: Overcoming the Barriers to Successful Utilization," *Management Review*, September 1969, pp. 9-14.

119. Bates, W.S. (Chapter 5, 44).

120. Batt, Christopher P. et al. (Chapter 2, SR, 1).

121. Batty, M. "Monitoring an Exponential Smoothing Forecasting System," *Operational Research Quarterly*, 20, No. 3 (September, 1969), pp. 319-25.

122. Benston, George J. "Multiple Regression Analysis of Cost Behavior," *The Accounting Review*, 41 (October, 1966), pp. 657-72.

123. Boulding, Kenneth E. "A Pure Theory of Conflict Applied to Organizations," in George Fisk (ed.). *The Frontiers of Management Psychology*. New York: Harper and Row Publishers Inc., 1964.

124. Couger, J.D., "Evolution of Business System Analysis Techniques," *Computing Survey*, Sept. 1973, pp. 167-98.

125. Dyment, John J. "Financial Planning with a Computer," *Financial Executive*, 28, No. 4 (April, 1970), p. 4.

126. Fient, H.G. (Chapter 4, SR, 1).

127. Gershefski, George W. "Building a Corporate Financial Model," *The Harvard Business Review*, 47 (July-August, 1969), pp. 61-72).

128. Greenberger, M. "The Priority Problem and Computer Time-Sharing," *Management Science*, 12, No. 11 (July, 1966), pp. 888-906.

129. Grinyer, Peter M., and Batt, Christopher (Chapter 2, 48).

130. Gross, Donald, and Ray, Jack L. "A General Purpose Forecased Simulator," *Management Science*, 11, No. 6 (April, 1965), pp. 119-35.

131. Hamilton, William F., and Moses, Michael A. "A Computer-Based Corporate Planning System," *Management Science* Vol. 12, No. 2 (October, 1974), pp. 148-59.

132. Hartley, Ronald V. "Some Extensions of Sensitivity Analysis," *The Accounting Review*, 45 (April, 1970), pp. 223-34.

133. Haskins, D. E., and Sliepcevich, C. M. "Invariant Principle of Control for Chemical Processes," *Industrial and Engineering Chemistry Fundamentals*, 4 (August, 1965), pp. 241-48.

134. Ishikawa, Akira. "Urban Problems and System Analysis (I)," *Urban Problems* (Japan), 58, No. 11 (1967).

135. _____. "Urban Problems and System Analysis (II)," *Urban Problems*, 58, No. 12 (1967).

136. ——, "Industrial Problems and System Engineering (I)," *Industrial Engineering* (Japan), November, 1967.

137. _____. "Industrial Problems and System Engineering (II)," *Industrial Engineering*, December, 1967.

138. _____. "Industrial Problems and System Engineering (III)," *Industrial Engineering*, January, 1968.

139. ——, "Management Information System and Planning, and Budgeting System," *Nippon Kogyo Shinbun*, October 10, 1969.

140. ——, and Smith, Charles H. "A Feedforward Control System for Organizational Planning and Control," Abacus, 8, No. 2 (December, 1972), pp. 163-80 and *International Studies of Management and Organization*, 3, No. 4 (Winter 1973-74), pp. 5-29.

141. Ishikawa, Akira, and Smith, Charles H. (Chapter 5, 38).

142. Ishikawa et al. (Chapter 2, 51).

143. Ishikawa, Akira and San Miguel, Joseph (Chapter 5, 31).

144. Ishikawa, Akira, (Chapter 6, 14).

145. Jaffe, J. "The System Design Phase, ed. by Perry E. Rosove, *Developing Computer-Based Information Systems*. New York: John Wiley and Sons, Inc., 1968.

146. Jensen, Robert E. "JENCAT Extensions: Prediction Models and Multivariate Analysis of Variance in Terms of Prediction Error," *Working Paper 72-10*, College of Business Administration, The University of Texas at Austin.

147. ———. "Sensitivity Analysis and Integer Linear Programming," *The Accounting Review*, 43 (July, 1968), pp. 425-46.

148. ———, "A Multiple Regression Model for Cost Control—Assumptions and Limitations," *The Accounting Review*, 41 (October, 1966), pp. 265-73.

149. Jewell, W. S. "Markov-Renewal Programming," *Operations Research*, 11 (November-December, 1963), pp. 938-71.

150. Jones, M. M. et al. (Chapter 4, SR, 3).

151. Kingston, P.L., "Concepts of Financial Models," *IBM Systems Journal*, 12, No. 2, 1973, pp. 113-25.

152. Khoury, E.N., and Nelson, H. Wayne, "Simulation in Financial Planning," *Management Services*, 2, No. 2 (March-April, 1965), pp. 13-21.

153. Kleinrock, L. "Analysis of a Time-Shared Processor," *Naval Research Logistics Quarterly*, 11, pp. 59-73.

154. ———. "Time-Shared Systems: A Theoretical Treatment," *JACM*, 14, pp. 242-61.

155. Koontz, Harold, and Bradspies, Robert W. "Managing through Feed-forward Control," *Business Horizons* (June, 1972), pp. 25-36.

156 Labovitz, Sanford I. "Criteria for Selecting a Significance Level: A Note on the Sacredness of .05," *American Sociologist*, 3 (1968), pp. 220-22.

157 Luyben, W. L., and Gerster, J. A. "Feed-forward Control of Distillation Columns," *Industrial and Engineering Chemistry Process Design and Development*, 3 (October, 1964), pp. 374-81.

158. MacMullan, E.C., and Shinskey, F.G. "Feed-forward Analog Computer Control of a Superfractionator," *Control Engineering*, 11 (March, 1964), 69-74.

159. McGuire, M. L. "Optimal Feedforward-Feedback Control of Dead Time Systems," *Industrial and Engineering Chemistry Fundamentals*, 8 (May, 1969), pp. 253-57.

160. Miller, Irvin M. "Computer Graphics for Decision Making," *The Harvard Business Review*, 47 (November-December, 1969), pp. 121-32.

161. Mitroff, Ian I. "A Communication Model of Dialectical Inquiring Systems—A Strategy for Strategic Planning" *Management Science*, 17, No. 10 (June, 1971) B-634-B-648.

162. Nanus, Burt. "The Multinational Computer," *Columbia Journal of World Business* (November-December, 1969), pp. 7-14.

163. Naylor, Thomas H., and Finger, J.M. (Chapter 2, 49).

164. Pryor, LeRoy J. "Simulation: Budgeting for a 'What If . . .'," *The Journal of Accountancy*, 130 (November, 1970), p. 60.

165. Rappaport, Alfred. "Sensitivity Analysis in Decision Making," *Accounting Review*, 42 (July, 1967), pp. 441-56.

166. San Miguel, Joseph, and Ishikawa, Akira (Chapter 5, 32).

167. Schneeweiss, Christoph A. "Smoothing Production by Inventory—An Application of the Wiener Filtering Theory," *Management Science*, 17, No. 7 (March, 1971), pp. 472-83.

168. Schrage, L.E. "The Queue M/G/1 with Feedback to Lower Priority Queus," *Management Science*, 13, No. 7 (March, 1967), pp. 566-74.

169. Schussel, George (Chapter 2, SR, 5).

170. Shinskey, F. G. "Feedforward Control Applied," *ISA Journal*, 10 (November, 1963), pp. 61-65.

171. Shostack, Kenneth, and Eddy, Charles. "Management by Computer Graphics," *The Harvard Business Review*, 49 (November-December, 1971), pp. 52-63.

172. Sibley, E.H., and Merten, A.G. (Chapter 5, SR, 4).

173. Ishikawa, Akira, and Smith, Charles H., "Feedforward Control in the Total Planning and Control System," *Cost and Management*, 46, No. 6 (November/December, 1972), pp. 36-41.

174. Sterling, Robert R. "On Theory Construction and Verification," *The Accounting Review*, 45 (July, 1970), pp. 444-57.

175. Teichroew, D., and Sayani, H. (Chapter 5, SR, 5).

176. Wagle, B. "The Use of Models for Environmental Forecasting and Corporate Planning," *Operational Research Quarterly*, 20, No. 3 (September, 1969), pp. 327-36.

177. Wagner, Wayne H., Akutagawa, Lawrence T., and Cuneo, Larry J. "Telecommunications Earnings Estimation Model (TEEM): An Evaluation," in Albert N. Schrieber, editor, *Corporate Simulation Models*. Seattle, Wash.: the University of Washington, 1970, pp. 396-430.

OTHER

178. Burford, Leslie Jeanne. Internal Analysis and Applications. Master's thesis, The University of Texas at Austin, August, 1968.

179. *Encyclopedia Dictionary of Systems and Procedures*. Prepared by the Prentice-Hall Editorial Staff. Englewood Cliffs, N. J.: Prentice-Hall, Inc., 1966.

180. Graham, Robert G., and Gray, Clifford F. *Business Games Handbook*. New York: American Management Association, 1969.

181. Griffith, Hugh Wallace. Preliminary Investigations Using Interval Arithmetic In the Numerical Evaluation of Polynomials. The University of Texas at Austin, dissertation, December, 1970.

182. Hibbs, R. F. "Dinner Address," at the 2nd Annual Conference of the Society of Management Information Systems. Washington, D.C.: Shoreham Hotel, September 14-15, 1970.

183. Ireson, W., and Grant, E. eds., *Handbook of Industrial Engineering and Management*. Englewood Cliffs, N.J.: Prentice-Hall, Inc., 1955.

184. Ishikawa, Akira. Cost-Effectiveness Analysis: Its Development, Present Status, and Potential Applications. Master's Thesis, the University of Washington, June, 1969.

185. Ishikawa, Akira. The Development of a Corporate Planning and Control Model. Doctoral Dissertation, The University of Texas at Austin, May, 1972.

186. Maynard, H.B., ed., *Handbook of Business Administration*. N.Y.: McGraw-Hill, 1967.

187. Patel, N. R. A Mathematical Analysis of Computer Time-Sharing Systems, M.S. Thesis, Department of Electrical Engineering, M.I.T., Cambridge, Mass., May, 1964.

188. Scherr, Allan L. An Analysis of Time-Shared Computer System. Doctoral Dissertation, Department of Electrical Engineering, M.I.T., June, 1965.

189. Science Service, ed. *Science New Year Book 1969/70*. New York: Science News, 1969.

INDEX

A

Abacus Electronics, 108, 110
activity structure, 16
adaptive planning and control, 83-84
adjustments during the process of
  development, 48
American Airlines, 60
American Institute of Electrical
  Engineers, 80
application of the model, 54
audio devices, 1
authority, 48

B

benefits from computerized corporate
  models, 63-75, 132-133
Boche, 105
Boeing Company, 24
bottom-up approach, 20-21, 130
Brandt, 20
breakeven analysis, 108-113
Bright, 67
Burroughs Corporate Simulation
  Model, 21
business games, 23

C

Chambers, Mullick, and Smith, 29, 52
Cobol, 32
computerized corporate planning
  models, 11-14
coordination, 48-49, 131-132
corporate financial models, 1, 4
corporate planning and control, 1
corporate planning and control
  models, 4
C. P. U. time cost, 74

D

data management, 29-33, 131
Dayton Hudson Corporation, 34
decision simulation, 23
decision tree, 45
design methods, 19-21, 130
Desmonde, 67
developing a corporate model, 43-56,
  131-132
Dynamo, 32

E

eclectic approach, 21, 130

163